THE LOW CARB HIGH FIBER COOKBOOK

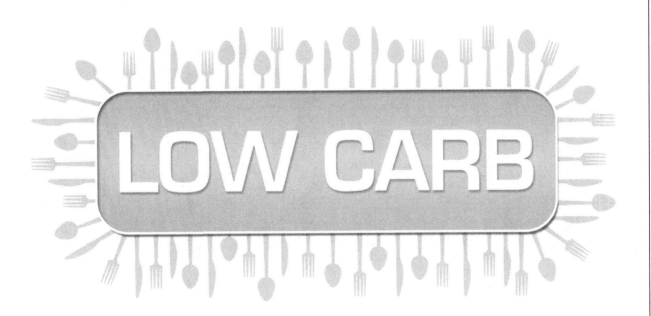

Eating Well and Losing Weight: A Guide to Healthy, Delicious, and Nutritious Easy-to-Make Low Carb High Fiber Recipes

Cameroon N. Brown

Table Of Contents

INTRODUCTION

The Low Carb High Fiber Cookbook is a collection of recipes created to assist those who want to increase their intake of dietary fiber while decreasing their consumption of carbs to enhance their general health and well-being. A group of culinary and nutrition professionals who have developed the cookbook has created a selection of delectable and simple-to-prepare meals that are both low in carbs and rich in fiber.

Breakfast, lunch, dinner, snacks, and desserts are just a few of the categories that make it simple for readers to locate the ideal dish for each meal of the day. Each dish comes with a list of ingredients, detailed directions, and dietary data.

The cookbook's recipes are designed to be wholesome and filling, making them ideal for anybody trying to get in shape, improve their digestion, or just eat a more well-rounded diet. A few of the recipes are:

Breakfast: Low-carb, high-fiber meal muffins

Lunch: Broccoli and cheddar soup with low carbs and high fiber

Snacks: include Low-carb, high-fiber zucchini fries

Dinner: Low-carb, high-fiber spaghetti squash bolognese.

Dessert: Low-carb, high-fiber chocolate chip cookies.

Anyone trying to enhance their diet and nutrition to improve their health and well-being should check out the Low Carb High Fiber Cookbook. It is a must-have for anybody trying to eat a healthy and balanced diet since it contains delectable, simple-to-make dishes that are rich in fiber and low in carbs.

The book also offers practical advice for cutting down on sugar and fat, as well as many meal ideas to ease your transition. This book will provide you with the direction and inspiration you need to make excellent and nourishing meals, whether you're a novice or an experienced chef.

CHAPTER ONE

UNDERSTANDING LOW-CARB, HIGH-FIBER DIETS

In a low-carb, high-fiber diet, the amount of carbs consumed is decreased while the amount of dietary fiber consumed is increased. This kind of diet is often used to improve overall health and lose weight.

Along with lipids and proteins, carbohydrates are one of the three macronutrients that our body utilizes as an energy source. Foods including bread, pasta, grains, fruits, and vegetables all contain them. Carbohydrates are transformed by the body into glucose, which is a source of energy.

The body will, however, store excess glucose as fat if it is given more than it requires. This may result in gaining weight and a higher chance of developing chronic illnesses like diabetes and heart disease.

The body cannot digest dietary fiber, which is a form of carbohydrate. It may be found in whole grains, legumes, fruits, and vegetables. Because it keeps the intestines regular and may help avoid constipation, fiber is crucial for keeping a healthy digestive tract. Additionally, it aids in lowering blood sugar and cholesterol levels, which may minimize the risk of diabetes and heart disease.

Foods that are low in carbs but rich in fiber include leafy green vegetables, berries, nuts, and seeds as part of a low-carb, high-fiber diet. Additionally, these foods are a good source of antioxidants, vitamins, and minerals, all of which are crucial for good health. On this kind of diet, foods like refined grains and added sugars that are heavy in carbs but low in fiber are usually restricted or avoided.

It's crucial to remember that a high-fiber, low-carb diet has to be balanced and shouldn't be followed for long periods. Too few carbs in the diet may result in deficits in vital elements such as vitamins, minerals, and fiber. It's essential to check that a low-carb, high-fiber diet is balanced and to talk with a healthcare professional before making any big dietary changes.

In conclusion, a low-carb, high-fiber diet may help with weight loss and general health enhancement. It is possible to encourage weight loss, lower the risk of developing chronic illnesses, and maintain stable blood sugar levels by consuming fewer carbs and more dietary fiber. Before making any significant dietary adjustments, it's crucial to ensure that a low-carb, high-fiber diet is balanced and to speak with a healthcare provider.

WHY LOW CARB-HIGH FIBER?

In recent years, low-carb, high-fiber diets have gained popularity as a means of shedding pounds and enhancing general health. These two dietary ingredients together may provide the body with some benefits.

Blood sugar levels may be regulated by a low-carb diet, which is one of its key benefits. In the body, carbohydrates are converted to glucose (sugar), which is then either utilized as fuel or stored as fat. Blood sugar levels may increase when the body absorbs more glucose than it requires, increasing the risk of diabetes and other chronic disorders. A low-carb diet may aid in weight loss and general health by stabilizing blood sugar levels by limiting the consumption of carbs.

A high-fiber diet is advantageous for both weight loss and general health. Fruits, vegetables, whole grains, and legumes contain fiber, a form of carbohydrate that the body cannot process. By making you feel full and content and so reducing cravings and overeating, a high-fiber diet may aid in weight loss. Additionally, it aids in lowering blood sugar and cholesterol levels, which may minimize the risk of diabetes and heart disease.

A diet rich in fiber may also help with regularity and digestion, and it may lower your chance of developing some diseases including colon cancer. Additionally, it helps with greater vitamin and mineral absorption and is good for intestinal health.

The promotion of nutrient-dense foods like fruits, vegetables, and whole grains, which are high in vitamins, minerals, and antioxidants, is another advantage of a low-carb, high-fiber diet. These meals may lower the chance of developing chronic illnesses like cancer and heart disease and are crucial for general health.

It's crucial to remember that a high-fiber, low-carb diet has to be balanced and shouldn't be followed for long periods. Too few carbs in the diet may result in deficits in vital elements such as vitamins, minerals, and fiber. Before making any significant dietary changes, it's also crucial to speak with a trained dietician or a healthcare provider.

As a result of controlling blood sugar levels, increasing weight loss, and lowering the risk of chronic illnesses, a low-carb, high-fiber diet may be advantageous for weight loss and general health. Additionally, it encourages eating nutrient-dense meals, which are crucial for good health and well-being in general. However, it should be balanced, and you should speak with a doctor before making any significant dietary changes.

HOW LOW-CARB AND HIGH-FIBER DIETS WORK

Diets which are high in fiber and low in carbohydrates function by consuming more fiber while consuming low carbohydrates. The body may experience several effects as a result, which may help with weight loss and general health.

- **Blood sugar control**: During digestion, carbohydrates are converted to glucose (sugar), which the body either uses as fuel or stores as fat. Blood sugar levels can increase when the body receives more glucose than it requires, increasing the risk of diabetes and other chronic diseases. A low-carb diet can help to maintain stable blood sugar levels by reducing the intake of carbohydrates, which can be advantageous for weight loss and general health.

- **Satiety**: Foods high in fiber tend to be more filling and may aid in satiety by reducing cravings and limiting overeating. Weight loss and weight control may result from this.

- **Cholesterol control**: Diets high in fiber may help decrease cholesterol, which can lessen the risk of heart disease. Particularly soluble fibers are recognized for their capacity to lower LDL cholesterol levels.

- **Digestion**: Fiber is crucial for keeping the digestive tract in good shape and may aid with constipation and other digestive problems.

- **Cancer prevention**: Consuming a lot of fiber may lower your chance of developing some cancers, such as colon cancer.

- **Vitamin and mineral absorption**: High fiber diets may aid in the absorption of vital vitamins and minerals, which is good for the health of the gut.

Too few carbs in the diet may result in deficits in vital elements such as vitamins, minerals, and fiber.

As a result, low-carb and high-fiber diets promote the consumption of more dietary fiber, which has several health benefits for the body, including the regulation of blood sugar, satiety, cholesterol, digestion, cancer prevention, and vitamin and mineral absorption. Before making any significant dietary adjustments, it's crucial to ensure that a low-carb, high-fiber diet is balanced and to speak with a healthcare provider.

For optimum health, one needs to eat a varied, balanced diet that is high in nutrient-dense foods. A well-rounded diet that includes a range of nutrient-dense meals is crucial for achieving optimum health, therefore it's also necessary to focus on the quality of food options rather than simply their macronutrient quantity.

BENEFITS OF EATING LOW-CARB HIGH-FIBER DIET

There are many benefits to eating a diet rich in fiber and low in carbs for general health and well-being. Among the key benefits are:

- **Weight Loss**: By maintaining stable blood sugar levels and making you feel satiated and full, a low-carb, high-fiber diet may aid in weight loss. Additionally, the high fiber content may aid in reducing cravings and limiting overeating.

- **Better Blood Sugar Control**: A low-carb, high-fiber diet may assist to manage blood sugar levels and lower the risk of developing diabetes by limiting the consumption of carbs.

- **Improved Heart Health**: A diet rich in fiber may help decrease blood pressure and cholesterol levels, which can lessen the risk of heart disease.

- **Improved Digestion**: Fiber may aid in preventing constipation and other digestive problems and is crucial for keeping a healthy digestive tract.

- **Reduced Risk of Specific Cancers**: Consuming a lot of fiber may lower the risk of specific cancers like colon cancer.

- **Better absorption of vitamins and minerals**: High-fiber diets are good for gut health and may aid in the absorption of vital vitamins and minerals.

- **Satiety**: Increasing satiety and decreasing appetite are two benefits of high-fiber diets that may aid in weight loss and weight maintenance.

- **Reduced Inflammation**: Low-carb diets may lower the body's inflammatory response, which can help lower the chance of developing chronic illnesses including cancer and heart disease.

It's crucial to remember that a high-fiber, low-carb diet has to be balanced and shouldn't be followed for long periods. Too few carbs in the diet may result in deficits in vital elements such as vitamins, minerals, and fiber. Before making any significant dietary changes, it's also crucial to speak with a trained dietician or a healthcare provider.

In conclusion, a diet rich in fiber and low in carbohydrates may provide a variety of benefits for general health and well-being. It may help to balance blood sugar levels, promote weight loss, enhance heart health, and digestion, lower the risk of certain malignancies, improve gut health, and boost satiety by consuming fewer carbs and more fiber. Before making any significant dietary adjustments, it's crucial to ensure that a low-carb, high-fiber diet is balanced and to speak with a healthcare provider.

TIPS FOR EATING LOW-CARB HIGH-FIBER DIET

A diet high in fiber and low in carbohydrates could be an excellent way to improve overall health and well-being. Take into account these ideas to get you going:

- **Plan ahead**: Make a meal plan in advance to assist you to ensure that you are receiving enough fiber and that your carbohydrate intake is under control. Planning your meals for the week and creating a list of high-fiber, low-carb things to purchase can assist with this.

- **Eat more vegies**: Increasing your vegetable intake may aid in weight loss since vegetables are low in carbohydrates and a great source of fiber. You should include a variety of vegetables in your diet, including leafy greens, broccoli, cauliflower, and Brussels sprouts.

- **Include healthy fats in your diet**: Fats are a crucial part of a balanced diet and may aid in satiation and fullness. The best sources of healthy fats include nuts, seeds, and avocados.

- **Choose whole grains**: Because they are a greater source of fiber and often have fewer carbohydrates, whole grains are preferable to processed grains. Examples of entire grains include quinoa, brown rice, and oats.

- **Limit processed foods**: since they may be low in fiber and high in added sugars and refined carbohydrates. Try to eat more whole, unprocessed foods, and less processed ones.

- **Drink enough water**: You need water for digestion, and drinking enough of it keeps you satisfied and full longer. Try to consume eight glasses of water or more each day.

- **Don't over eat**: Eat when you are hungry and stop eating when you are full by paying attention to your levels of hunger and fullness. Your body will communicate what it needs.

- **Get enough sleep**: not doing so might affect your appetite and cravings. For overall good health and well-being, sleep is essential. Sleep for 7-8 hours every night if you can.

- **Consult a professional**: You shouldn't stick to a well-balanced, high-fiber, low-carb diet for an extended length of time. It's essential to consult a licensed dietitian or healthcare professional before making any substantial dietary adjustments.

In conclusion, eating a diet high in fiber and low in carbs may have several positive effects on your overall health and happiness. By following these recommendations, you can make sure that you are getting enough fiber and that your carbohydrate intake is under control. It's essential to check that a low-carb, high-fiber diet is balanced and to talk with a healthcare professional before making any big dietary changes.

SHOPPING FOR LOW-CARB, HIGH-FIBER FOOD

It can be a little difficult to shop for low-carb, high-fiber foods, but with the right strategy, it's not impossible. The following advice will assist you in choosing low-carb, high-fiber foods:

- **Plan ahead**: Make a grocery list of the high-fiber, low-carb foods you'll need and schedule your meals in advance. This will enable you to maintain focus and prevent impulsive purchases.

- **Shop the perimeter**: The fresh meats, produce, and dairy products are located around the outside of the supermarket. These foods typically contain a lot of fiber and a few carbohydrates.

- **Verify labels**: Make sure to read the food labels before purchasing them and take note of the carbohydrate and fiber content. Look for foods that are low in carbohydrates and high in fiber.

- **Choose whole foods**: Whole foods, such as fruits, vegetables, nuts, and seeds, are often rich in fiber and low in carbs. Try to prefer whole foods over processed ones whenever you can.

- **Choose lean proteins**: Go for lean meats like fish, poultry, and beef. These have a lot of protein and little carbs.

- **Avoid added sugars**: Added sugars are frequently present in processed foods and they raise the risk of developing chronic diseases as well as weight gain. Search for foods with little added sugar.

- **Try new foods**: Many delectable and nutritious foods are high in fiber and low in carbohydrates. Try out new foods like spaghetti squash, zucchini noodles, or cauliflower rice.

- **Consult a specialist**: A balanced low-carb, high-fiber diet shouldn't be followed for prolonged periods. Before making any significant dietary changes, it's important to speak with a registered dietitian or a healthcare provider.

Buying low-carb, high-fiber food can be a little difficult, but with the right strategy, it can be done with ease. You can make sure that you are getting enough fiber and controlling your carbohydrate intake by pre-planning, shopping the perimeter, reading labels, choosing whole foods, choosing lean proteins, avoiding added sugars, experimenting with new foods, and talking to a professional. Before making any significant dietary changes, it's crucial to ensure that a low-carb, high-fiber diet is balanced and to speak with a healthcare provider.

CHAPTER TWO

COMPARISON WITH OTHER DIETS

Similar to other kinds of diets, low-carb and high-fiber diets emphasize making better dietary choices to enhance general health and well-being. Low-carb, high-fiber diets vary significantly from other kinds of diets in a few important ways.

- **Low-carb diets**: Low-carb diets like the ketogenic diet and the Atkins diet place a strong emphasis on restricting the consumption of carbs. However, increasing fiber consumption may not always be a priority on low-carb diets.

- **High-protein diets**: High-protein diets, like the Dukan diet, emphasize boosting protein consumption while lowering carbohydrate intake. High-protein diets, like low-carb and high-fiber ones, may aid in weight loss and enhance general health.

- **Low-fat diets**: Low-fat diets, like the Ornish diet, emphasize cutting down on fat while increasing carbohydrate and fiber consumption.

They may not be as stringent as low-carb and high-fiber diets, but they nevertheless can aid in weight loss and enhance general health.

- **Plant-based diets**: Plant-based eating plans, like the Mediterranean diet, emphasize increasing the consumption of fruits, vegetables, whole grains, and legumes while lowering the consumption of animal products. Similar to low-carb and high-fiber diets, they are often rich in fiber and low in carbs.

Here is a comparison of the effectiveness of various diets and low-carb, high-fiber diets:

- **Low Fat vs. Low Carb**: Low-fat diets concentrate on cutting down on fats, whilst low-carb diets concentrate on cutting back on carbs. While both kinds of diets may help you lose weight, low carbohydrate diets may be more efficient at lowering your chance of developing certain chronic illnesses and improving blood sugar management.

- **Low Carb vs. Keto**: A low-carb diet that is heavy in fat is the ketogenic diet. The macronutrient ratio is the primary distinction between the keto and low-carb diets. While the keto diet is a very low-carb, high-fat diet that may restrict carbohydrate consumption to as little as 5% of daily calories, low-carb diets normally concentrate on limiting the intake of carbs to approximately 20–50 grams per day.

- **Low Carb vs. Mediterranean**: The Mediterranean diet is high in fresh produce, healthy grains, and lean meats. In that it is low in refined carbs, it is comparable to the low-carb diet, but it has more carbohydrates overall. Olive oil, one of the heart-healthy fats found in abundance in the Mediterranean diet, is another.

- **High Fiber vs. High Protein**: High fiber diets emphasize increasing dietary fiber consumption, while high protein diets emphasize increasing protein intake. Both diets may aid in weight loss and enhance general health, but high-fiber diets may be more efficient in terms of enhancing digestion, decreasing cholesterol and blood sugar levels, and lowering the chance of developing certain malignancies.

- **High Fiber vs. High Carb**: While high-carb diets emphasize increasing the consumption of carbs, high-fiber diets emphasize increasing the intake of dietary fiber. For those who require a lot of energy or are athletes, high-carb diets may be advantageous, but for the majority of individuals, a high-fiber diet is advised due to its positive effects on digestion, blood sugar control, and cancer prevention.

Diets rich in fiber and low in carbohydrates need to be balanced, and they shouldn't be followed for long periods. They are distinct from other diets including low-fat, ketogenic, Mediterranean, high-protein, and high-carbohydrate diets, each of which may offer certain benefits.

In conclusion, it's important to remember that, despite their potential for helping people lose weight and improve their general health, low-carb and high-fiber diets may not be appropriate for everyone. Before making any substantial dietary changes, it is always advised to seek the advice of a healthcare provider or a trained dietician. A well-rounded diet that includes a range of nutrient-dense foods is crucial for achieving optimum health, therefore it's vital to focus on the quality of food options rather than simply their macronutrient amount. It is crucial to remember that low-carb diets may cause dietary shortages if they are not followed correctly and over an extended period.

NUTRITIONAL VALUES

The most important nutrients to look for in low-carb high-fiber foods are dietary fiber, protein, healthy fats, and complex carbohydrates. These diets have been shown to provide several nutritional benefits, such as better blood sugar management, weight loss, and a lower chance of developing certain chronic illnesses.

Dietary fiber helps you feel fuller for extended periods and is essential for digestive health. Protein gives energy and aids in the development and maintenance of muscular mass. In addition to being necessary for appropriate hormone and brain function, healthy fats are critical for supplying energy. Complex carbs provide you with long-lasting energy and help keep your blood sugar levels steady.

An overview of the nutritional benefits of a low-carb, high-fiber diet is given below:

- **Low Carbs**: Diets low in carbohydrates, which are present in foods like grains, fruits, and sweets, limit the consumption of these nutrients. This may result in a decrease in daily caloric consumption, aiding in weight loss.

- **High Fiber**: A high-fiber diet includes more high-fiber foods, such as fruits, vegetables, nuts, seeds, and legumes. These meals may help suppress hunger and encourage weight loss since they are more satisfying than low-fiber foods.

- **High in protein**: Protein is a crucial food for maintaining bone strength, the muscular mass, and general health. To avoid muscle loss and promote satiety, a low-carb, high-fiber diet often contains a moderate to a high amount of protein from foods like meat, chicken, fish, and eggs.

- **Healthy Fats**: Diets rich in fiber and low in carbohydrates may also include healthy fats from foods like olive oil, avocado, nuts, and seeds. These fats may aid in weight loss and are crucial for preserving heart health. They can also increase satiety.

- **Low in added sugar**: Diets rich in fiber and low in carbohydrates often include less added sugar, which helps lower the risk of developing chronic illnesses including diabetes, obesity, and heart disease.

- **Nutrient-dense**: Providing a decent mix of necessary vitamins, minerals, and other nutrients, low-carb, high-fiber diets are often nutrient-dense.

Foods high in fiber and low in carbs are also nutrient-dense. They often include significant levels of calcium, magnesium, potassium, and iron. Potassium aids in the control of blood pressure and the contraction of muscles. Magnesium aids in the reduction of inflammation and is crucial for healthy bones. Iron aids in the formation of red blood cells and aids in controlling cell division and growth. For healthy bones and teeth as well as to control muscular contractions, calcium is crucial.

In conclusion, a diet that emphasizes foods that are rich in fiber and low in carbs is known as a low-carb, high-fiber diet. These diets have been shown to provide several nutritional benefits, such as better blood sugar management, weight loss, and a lower chance of developing certain chronic illnesses. A diet rich in fiber and low in carbs may provide a good mix of vitamins, minerals, and other nutrients. This is accomplished by eating foods that are high in fiber, protein, and healthy fats.

IMPORTANCE OF NUTRIENT BALANCE

For their health benefits, such as weight loss and better blood sugar management, low-carb, high-fiber diets are gaining popularity since they assist to lower total carbohydrate consumption while boosting the intake of fiber. It is crucial to remember that these diets also need a proper dietary balance to be healthy. A low-carb, high-fiber diet might result in dietary deficits, which can have major health repercussions if there is an improper nutrient balance.

Fatigue, headaches, and other symptoms may result from a diet that is too low in carbohydrates, which are a crucial source of energy for the body. Deficits in vital elements like vitamin B and minerals like iron and zinc may also result from eliminating whole food categories, such as grains. To make sure you are receiving all the nutrients you need, it is crucial to take a multivitamin. You may assist ensure that you are receiving enough of these important nutrients by taking a multivitamin.

Contrarily, fiber is crucial for keeping the digestive system in good shape and may help lower the risk of heart disease, diabetes, and several forms of cancer. It's crucial to remember, however, that if a diet rich in fiber is not balanced out by a sufficient consumption of water and other fluids, it may also result in an increased risk of constipation.

Eating a variety of nutrient-dense meals is the most crucial aspect of attaining a correct nutritional balance on a low-carb, high-fiber diet. This includes a range of colorful vegetables, lean proteins like fish, chicken, and eggs, healthy fats like olive oil and avocados, and whole grains like quinoa, oats, and buckwheat that are high in nutrients. You can make sure you are receiving a broad range of important nutrients, such as vitamins, minerals, and healthy fats, by eating a variety of meals.

While still limiting the consumption of carbohydrates and increasing the intake of fiber, this will help the body get the nutrients it needs to operate effectively.

Finally, it's crucial to stay hydrated when eating a low-carb, high-fiber diet. Your body needs water to be hydrated and to rid itself of pollutants. Constipation, a typical side effect of low-carb, high-fiber diets, may also be avoided with its aid.

You may maintain a good nutritional balance on a low-carb, high-fiber diet by consuming a variety of nutrient-dense foods, taking a multivitamin, and drinking plenty of water. This will guarantee that you are consuming all the nutrients required to maintain good health and a healthy weight.

Before beginning a low-carb, high-fiber diet, it's also a good idea to speak with a registered dietitian or other healthcare experts. They can help you customize the diet to meet your requirements and make sure you're receiving all the nutrients you need.

In conclusion, a low-carb, high-fiber diet may help with weight loss and blood sugar regulation, but it's crucial to make sure it's well-balanced in terms of other crucial nutrients. You may make sure that your body is receiving the nutrients it needs to operate correctly by incorporating a range of nutrient-dense meals and talking to a healthcare practitioner.

CHAPTER THREE

MEAL PLANNING AND PREPARATION

Meal planning and preparing while following a low-carb, high-fiber diet will help you shed pounds, control your blood sugar levels, and enhance your general health. A low-carb, high-fiber diet is a style of eating that emphasizes cutting down on carbs while increasing fiber intake. People with diabetes, those attempting to reduce weight, and those with other health issues are often advised to follow this kind of diet.

Planning meals for a low-carb, high-fiber diet requires paying special attention to nutrient-dense foods. This comprises complete grains, complex carbs, lean proteins, healthy fats, fruits, and vegetables. These foods are ideal for this kind of diet since they naturally include a lot of fiber and a few carbs. It's also important to limit additional sugars and processed foods.

Some examples of **Lean proteins** that can be included in a low-carb, high-fiber diet include:

- Chicken thigh
- Poultry breast
- Fish

- Tofu
- Eggs

Healthy fats to take in include:
- Nuts and seeds avocado
- Coconut oil
- Olive oil

Non-starchy vegetables that are high in fiber include:
- Slender leaves
- Broccoli
- Cauliflower
- Spinach
- Kale

Focus on cooking techniques that don't add excess fat or calories while preparing meals for a low-carb, high-fiber diet. Cooking techniques that are nutritious include roasting, sautéing, stir-frying, grilling, or baking. Additionally, it's crucial to pay attention to portion sizes since it's simple to eat more carbs than you meant to. To enhance taste without adding more fat or calories, you may also use herbs and spices.

Focus on nutrient-dense breakfast options including egg white omelets with veggies, Greek yogurt with nuts and fruit, and oatmeal with fruit and nuts. A salad with lean protein and a high-fiber grain, such as quinoa or barley, is a fantastic choice for lunch. Dinner ideas include lean meats and veggies that have been roasted or grilled.

On a diet rich in fiber and low in carbohydrates, snacks should be limited to fruits, nuts, seeds, berries, and whole-grain crackers or pieces of bread. Organizing and preparing snacks in advance is also a smart move. Always keep in mind to remain hydrated by sipping on the water often during the day.

Overall, meal planning and preparation on a high-fiber, low-carb diet may be a terrific strategy to enhance general health and meet weight loss objectives. Nutrient-dense meals, healthful cooking techniques, and drinking enough water should all be prioritized. These suggestions may be used to prepare scrumptious and healthy meals that will aid in your pursuit of better health.

BENEFITS OF MEAL PLANNING AND PREPARATION

As they may provide several benefits, meal planning and preparation are crucial for keeping a healthy and balanced low-carb, high-fiber diet. You may enhance your energy levels, lower your chance of developing chronic diseases, and maintain a healthy weight with its assistance.

Some of the main benefits of meal planning and preparation for a low-carb, high-fiber diet are listed below:

- **Improved Weight Management**: By giving you the proper ratio of nutrients, meal planning, and preparation for a low-carb, high-fiber diet may assist you in maintaining a healthy weight. Consuming a diet high in fiber might help you feel fuller for longer while consuming fewer calories overall.

- **Reduced Chance of Chronic Disease**: By giving your body the vitamins and minerals it needs, a low-carb, high-fiber diet may help lower your risk of developing chronic illnesses like diabetes, heart disease, and certain kinds of cancer. Because it helps with digestion, lowers cholesterol, and regulates blood sugar levels, fiber is a crucial part of a balanced diet and may lessen your chance of developing these illnesses.

- **Improved blood sugar control**: By consuming less total carbs overall and more fiber, a low-carb, high-fiber diet may aid in better blood sugar regulation. Meal preparation and planning might make it simpler to adhere to this kind of diet, which over time may result in better blood sugar management.

- **Intake of vital nutrients**: Including lean proteins, healthy fats, and non-starchy vegetables may be increased with the aid of meal planning and preparation. These foods are ideal for a low-carb, high-fiber diet because they are both naturally low in carbs and rich in fiber.

- **Improved Energy Levels**: A diet rich in fiber and low in carbohydrates may also help you feel more energized. You may obtain the boost of energy you need to get through the day by eating a diet high in fiber, which helps to keep your blood sugar levels constant.

- **Stress reduction**: By making it simpler to choose healthy options, meal planning and preparation may assist to decrease stress. It may be simpler to adhere to your diet if there are plenty of healthy alternatives accessible, which helps lessen the stress associated with making food decisions.

- **Enhanced efficiency**: By making it simpler to choose healthy options, meal planning and preparation may assist to amplify efficiency. It might be simpler to keep to your diet when there are convenient healthy alternatives accessible, which can ultimately save time.

- **Better Budgeting**: By purchasing goods in bulk and planning how to utilize them effectively, meal planning and preparation may also help you keep tabs on your spending. Long-term financial savings are possible thanks to this.

As they may provide you with several benefits, meal planning and preparation are crucial for keeping a healthy and balanced low-carb, high-fiber diet. It may assist with better blood sugar control, better budgeting, higher nutritional intake, less stress, enhanced productivity, and weight management in addition to lowering the chance of developing chronic diseases.

It can also aid with energy levels. You can make sure you have wholesome, nutrient-dense alternatives on hand and make smart decisions that will help you reach your health goals by taking the time to plan and prepare your meals in advance. Therefore, take into account meal planning and preparation on a low-carb high-fiber diet if you want to make a beneficial adjustment in your diet.

TIPS FOR MEAL PLANNING AND PREPARATION

Maintaining a low-carb, high-fiber diet requires careful meal planning and preparation, and there are a few tricks that might make the process simpler and more effective. Here are some pointers for organizing and cooking meals when following a low-carb, high-fiber diet:

- **Plan ahead**: Spend some time organizing your meals and snacks for the next week so that you can make sure you always have wholesome, nutrient-dense alternatives on hand. By doing this, you may be able to avoid overeating or selecting unhealthier options.

- **Make a grocery list**: Based on your meal plan, make a grocery list to make sure you have everything you need to prepare wholesome, nutrient-dense meals.

- **Choose High-Fiber Foods**: A low-carb, high-fiber diet requires the consumption of high-fiber foods. Be on the lookout for whole grains, nuts, seeds, and legumes. Consume a lot of fruits and veggies to obtain more fiber.

- **Cook in bulk**: Plan meals and snacks in excess so that you have leftovers for the rest of the week. This may help you save time and stick to your diet more easily.

- **Use healthy cooking techniques**: Concentrate on quick and healthy cooking techniques including grilling, roasting, and sautéing. Avoid culinary techniques like deep frying that add extra fat or calories.

- **Be Creative with Recipes**: Many delectable recipes are rich in fiber and low in carbohydrates. Plan your meals in a unique way and experiment with different dishes. Look for meals that are flavorful and made with natural ingredients.

- **Add variety**: Include a range of nutrient-dense foods in your diet, such as non-starchy veggies, lean meats, and healthy fats. By doing this, you may assist your body get the nutrients it needs to operate normally while still consuming fewer carbohydrates and more fiber.

- **Concentrate on Whole Meals**: Opt for minimally processed foods that are as near to their unprocessed forms as you can. Be sure to choose entire foods such as fruits, vegetables, lean meats, and healthy fats. Avoid refined sugars, trans fats, and processed meals.

- **Limit Added Sweets**: On a low-carb, high-fiber diet, added sugars may rapidly add up. As plain yogurt, almonds, and dark chocolate are minimal in added sugars.

- **Portion control**: Portion control is critical for all diets, but it's crucial for low-carb, high-fiber ones in particular. Be mindful of how much you are eating and refrain from overindulging.

- **Utilize leftovers**: Utilize leftovers rather than discard them. This may help you keep to your food plan while also saving you time and money.

- **Use Healthy Fats**: A low-carb, high-fiber diet must include healthy fats. Pick unsaturated fats like those found in almonds, avocados, and olive oil. Avoid unhealthy fats including saturated and trans fats.

- **Keep it simple**: Keep it simple and concentrate on nutrient-dense, complete foods rather than worrying about preparing elaborate meals.

- **Drink Lots of Water**: Maintaining a balanced diet and weight loss need you to stay hydrated. Try to consume eight to ten glasses of water daily.

- **Prepare more**: Make extra servings when you prepare so you have leftovers for subsequent meals. You won't have to prepare every meal from scratch, which will save you time and energy.

- **Get Enough Sleep**: Sleep is essential for maintaining good health. Spend 7-9 hours each night getting a good night's sleep.

- **Seek expert advice**: To help you customize the diet to your unique requirements and make sure you're receiving all the nutrients you need, speak with a registered dietitian or other healthcare professionals.

In conclusion, meal preparation and planning are crucial for maintaining a well-balanced low-carb, high-fiber diet, and these suggestions may make the process simpler and more effective. You may plan and prepare meals that are rich in fiber and low in carbohydrates by using the advice in this article. It could take some getting accustomed to, but with enough effort, you can cook delicious meals that are healthy and will help you achieve your health objectives.

CHAPTER FOUR

LOW-CARB HIGH-FIBER RECIPES

Recipes with high fiber content and low carbs are a fantastic approach to boosting overall health and well-being while still enjoying delicious and filling meals. You might try the following examples of low-carb, high-fiber recipes:

- Breakfast muffins that are high in fiber and low in carbohydrates may be produced with flaxseed meal, almond flour, and coconut flour. They are a fantastic choice for a quick breakfast on the run.

- Broccoli and cheddar soup with low carbs and high fiber is a tasty and satisfying dish that is ideal for lunch or supper. It contains broccoli, cheddar cheese, and heavy cream, and is low in carbs and rich in fiber.

- This dish is a fantastic low-carb substitute for regular spaghetti and meat sauce. Low Carb High Fiber Spaghetti Squash Bolognese It is a tasty and filling dinner that utilizes spaghetti squash in place of pasta and a high-fiber beef sauce.

- Zucchini fries with high fiber and low carbs are a fantastic low-carb substitute for regular fries. They are prepared using zucchini and baked as a healthier alternative to frying.

- Low Carb High Fiber Chocolate Chip Cookies: If you have a sweet taste, these cookies are a delightful and gratifying treat. They are low in carbs and rich in fiber since they are created with sugar-free chocolate chips, almond flour, and coconut flour.

It's crucial to remember that a high-fiber, low-carb diet has to be balanced and shouldn't be followed for long periods. Too few carbs in the diet may result in deficits in vital elements such as vitamins, minerals, and fiber. Before making any significant dietary changes, it's also crucial to speak with a trained dietician or a healthcare provider.

In conclusion, a diet rich in fiber and low in carbohydrates may provide a variety of benefits for general health and well-being. These are some examples of tasty and filling low-carb, high-fiber meals that you may try. They provide adequate fiber while minimizing your consumption of carbs. Before making any significant dietary adjustments, it's crucial to ensure that a low-carb, high-fiber diet is balanced and to speak with a healthcare provider.

ADJUSTING RECIPES TO FIT DIETARY RESTRICTIONS

Diets rich in fiber and low in carbohydrates are becoming more and more well-liked as a strategy to shed weight and improve general health. A low-carb, high-fiber diet may be a terrific way to continue enjoying your favorite foods while still eating healthily, but it can be difficult to adapt recipes to match dietary constraints. Here are some suggestions for modifying your go-to meals so they adhere to a low-carb, high-fiber diet.

1. Choose low-carb, high-fiber ingredients: While some carbohydrates are essential for a healthy diet, most persons on a low-carb diet should seek to minimize their intake of carbohydrates. Choose low-carb, high-fiber items for your dishes, such as veggies, nuts & seeds, and legumes.

2. **Make use of low-carb sweeteners**: If a recipe asks for a sweetener, choose one with a high fiber content and a few carbohydrates. Erythritol, stevia, and monk fruit extract are a few of the more well-liked alternatives.

3. **Replace high-carb ingredients with low-carb alternatives**: Substitute low-carb components for high-carb ones when a recipe asks for them. Examples of low-carb substitutes for high-carb ingredients include almond flour, cauliflower rice, and monk fruit essence.

4. **Increase the number of non-starchy veggies**: Adding more non-starchy vegetables to a meal might make a dish have fewer carbohydrates while adding more fiber and minerals. For instance, increasing the amount of spinach, broccoli, or cauliflower in a meal might increase its fiber and nutritional value while lowering its carbohydrate content.

5. **Add more fiber**: Increase the fiber content of a meal by including additional veggies and/or legumes. For instance, add more beans and chopped veggies while cooking soup.

6. **Add healthy fats**: Including healthy fats will help you stay content and full while also supplying vital nutrients. Examples of good fats include avocados, nuts, seeds, and olive oil.

7. **Experiment with various herbs and spices**: Using different herbs and spices may help you flavor your food without adding additional calories or carbohydrates.

8. **Reduce portion sizes**: To adhere to your dietary limits, it can be essential to scale down portions of dishes that are especially high in carbohydrates.

9. **Consult with a professional**: To customize the recipe to your unique requirements and make sure you're receiving all the nutrients you need, speak with a registered dietitian or a healthcare expert.

You may prepare tasty, low-carb, high-fiber recipes that adhere to your dietary constraints by using the advice in this article. You may develop foods you like while still adhering to your dietary objectives if you put a little ingenuity into it.

OVERVIEW OF RECIPE TYPES

Low-carb high-fiber recipes are increasing in popularity as more people explore methods to consume fewer carbohydrates while still eating delectable food. For meals that are filling and delicious, low-carb high-fiber recipes mix high-fiber foods with low-carb items.

Dishes rich in fiber and low in carbohydrates often have fewer calories and more fiber than conventional recipes. Together, these factors may make individuals feel satisfied for longer and lower their chance of becoming obese. Furthermore, compared to conventional recipes, these dishes often use less processed foods, which may aid to improve general health.

The best recipes for anybody trying to consume fewer carbohydrates but still obtain a lot of fiber are those that are low in carbohydrates. A low-carb diet might benefit greatly from the diversity that these meals can bring. There are many delectable meals with low carbs and high fiber to select from, from breakfast to supper.

Recipe options for a low-carb, high-fiber diet might range from main dishes to sides to snacks and desserts. An overview of some of the several recipe categories that may be used in a low-carb, high-fiber diet is provided below:

- **Main dishes**: There are several possibilities for main dishes, including meat, fish, poultry, and vegetarian options. Grilled chicken breast with a side of roasted vegetables, salmon with a side salad, or a vegetable stir-fry with tofu are a few examples of low-carb, high-fiber main dishes.

- **Sides**: Non-starchy vegetables such as leafy greens, broccoli, cauliflower, and Brussels sprouts are examples of sides. These may be cooked in many ways, such as roasting, sautéing, or steaming, and they can be served with a main dish to increase the amount of fiber and nutrients in a meal.

- **Snacks**: A range of foods, such as nuts, seeds, berries, and non-starchy vegetables like carrots or celery, may be consumed as snacks. To aid with appetite control and as a source of fiber, they may be enjoyed as a nutritious alternative in between meals.

- **Desserts**: By using replacement components such as sugar alternatives, low-carb flour, and nut butter, desserts may be enjoyed while adhering to a low-carb, high-fiber diet. Examples include low-carb chocolate chip cookies, sugar-free and low-carb cheesecake, and berry sorbet.

- **Soups and stews**: Adding non-starchy veggies to a low-carb, high-fiber diet via soups and stews might be a terrific idea. They are a wonderful way to have a hearty and warming supper and can be cooked with a variety of veggies and lean meats.

- **Salads**: Salads may be eaten as a main meal or a side dish and are a fantastic way to obtain your daily serving of non-starchy veggies. Lean meats like grilled chicken or shrimp and a variety of greens and vegetables may be used to make them.

- **Smoothies**: Smoothies are a fantastic low-carb, high-fiber breakfast or snack choice. Various components, including leafy greens, berries, nuts, seeds, and non-starchy vegetables, may be used to make them. While keeping the carbohydrate amount low, these nutrients may serve as a healthy source of fiber, vitamins, and minerals.

- **One-pot dinners and casseroles**: One-pot meals and casseroles may be a terrific method to simplify meal preparation and planning. They can be created using a range of ingredients that are rich in fiber and low in carbohydrates. Vegetables, lean meats, and healthy fats are just a few of the components that may be used to make casseroles and one-pot dinners.

- **Sandwiches and wraps**: By utilizing substitute items like lettuce leaves or low-carb wraps and lean meats and non-starchy veggies as fillings, sandwiches and wraps may also be a terrific way to enjoy a low-carb, high-fiber diet.

- **Breakfast options**: A range of foods, including eggs, nuts, seeds, and non-starchy vegetables, may be used to make breakfast options. While keeping the carbohydrate amount low, these nutrients may serve as a healthy source of fiber, vitamins, and minerals.

In conclusion, a diet rich in fiber and low in carbohydrates may contain a wide range of food types, including main dishes, sides, snacks, desserts, soups and stews, salads, smoothies, casseroles, one-pot meals, sandwiches and wraps, and breakfast options. It may be simple to follow a low-carb, high-fiber diet and eat scrumptious, healthful meals by using a range of products and dish types.

RECIPES AND INGREDIENTS

A low-carb, high-fiber diet may include a wide variety of recipes and ingredients. The secret is to incorporate a mix of meals that are rich in fiber and low in carbs.

Some examples of recipes rich in fiber and low in carbohydrates might contain the following meals and ingredients:

- **Lean protein recipes**: Lean proteins, such as chicken, fish, turkey, and tofu, may be a terrific method to provide your body the nutrition it needs while lowering the number of carbohydrates in a recipe.

- **Non-starchy vegetables**: Non-starchy vegetables such as leafy greens, broccoli, cauliflower, and Brussels sprouts, are excellent sources of fiber and nutrients. They may be used in a range of dishes, including soups, stews, salads, and casseroles.

- **Healthy fats**: Healthy fats may be used in dishes to enhance taste and texture while also supplying necessary nutrients, such as olive oil, avocado, nuts, and seeds.

- **Nuts and seeds**: Nuts and seeds may be used as a snack or in recipes to provide taste and texture as well as beneficial fats, fiber, and protein.

- **Low-carb flours**: Low-carb flours may be used in recipes as a low-carb substitute for wheat flour. Examples include almond flour, coconut flour, and flaxseed meal.

- **Sugar alternatives**: Sugar alternatives like erythritol, stevia, and xylitol may be added to recipes to lower the total amount of sugar while keeping the recipe's sweetness.

- **Herbs and spices**: Herbs and spices may be used to flavor food without adding additional calories or carbohydrates.

- **Berries**: Berries may be utilized in desserts, smoothies, and snacks since they are a fantastic source of fiber and antioxidants.

- **Eggs**: Eggs are a fantastic source of protein and can be used in a wide range of recipes, including soups, salads, and casseroles as well as breakfast foods.

- **Low-carb dairy products**: To add flavor and richness to meals, low-carb dairy products like cheese, yogurt, and heavy cream may be utilized.

To keep hydrated and aid in the body's digestion of fiber, it is crucial to drink plenty of water throughout the day.

In addition to all the complete meals, you may also include low-carb fruits and veggies, protein bars, and shakes as healthy snacks.

Incorporating a lot of fiber-rich, whole meals and nutritious snacks is essential for a low-carb, high-fiber diet to be effective. You may do this to keep yourself fulfilled, satiated, and healthy.

In conclusion, a low-carb, high-fiber diet may contain a range of tasty, wholesome, and simple meals and components. You can make sure you are getting all the essential nutrients while also maintaining a low carbohydrate intake and a high fiber intake by including lean proteins, non-starchy vegetables, healthy fats, low-carb flours, sugar substitutes, spices and herbs, berries, nuts, seeds, eggs, and low-carb dairy products in your diet.

This kind of diet may provide several health benefits, including weight loss, better blood sugar regulation, and a lower chance of developing certain chronic illnesses. Using these components and experimenting with other recipe categories, such as main dishes, sides, snacks, and desserts, may also simplify meal planning and preparation. You may enjoy tasty and healthful meals while simultaneously attaining your health objectives with a balanced and well-planned low-carb, high-fiber diet.

THE RECIPES

BREAKFAST RECIPES

Kale and Egg Breakfast Bowl

Ingredients: **Prep time**: 10 minutes

- 2 big eggs,
- 2 cups of chopped kale,
- ¼ cup of diced bell pepper and onion,

- 2 teaspoons of extra virgin olive oil, and
- ¼ teaspoon of garlic powder.
- Salt and pepper are added to taste.

Preparation: **Preparation time**: 15 minutes

- Over medium heat, warm the olive oil in a large skillet.
- While cooking for 5 minutes, mix in the onion and bell pepper.
- Stirring periodically, simmer the chopped kale for a further 5 minutes after adding the garlic powder, salt, and pepper.
- Add the eggs and cook for 3 to 4 minutes, depending on how done you want your eggs.
- In a bowl, dish up, and savor.

Avocado Toast

Ingredients: **Prep time**: 5 minutes

- 2 pieces of whole grain bread,
- ½ a ripe avocado,
- 2 tablespoons of feta cheese,
- ¼ teaspoon of garlic powder, and
- Salt and pepper to taste.

Preparation: **Preparation time:** 2 minutes

- Toast the bread until it is just beginning to turn golden then sprinkle the avocado on top.
- Add feta cheese, garlic powder, salt, and pepper to taste. Enjoy.

A parfait of Greek yogurt

Ingredients: **Prep time**: 5 minutes

- 1 tablespoon honey,
- 2 tablespoons chopped walnuts,
- 1/2 cup plain Greek yogurt,
- 1/4 cup fresh berries.

Preparation: **Preparation time**: 2 minutes

- In a parfait glass, arrange the Greek yogurt, fresh fruit, almonds, and honey. Enjoy.

Egg and cheese sandwich

Ingredients: **Prep time**: 10 minutes

- 2 pieces of whole grain bread,
- 2 big eggs,
- 2 slices of low-fat cheese, and
- 1 tablespoon of olive oil.

Preparation: **Preparation time**: 5 minutes

- Over medium heat, warm the olive oil in a large skillet.
- Add the eggs and cook for 3 to 4 minutes, depending on how done you want your eggs.
- Put the cheese on top and sandwich the eggs between the 2 pieces of bread.
- Toast until the cheese is melted in a toaster or a pan. Enjoy.

Veggie Omelet

Ingredients: **Prep time**: 10 minutes

- 2 big eggs,
- 1/4 cup each chopped bell pepper, onion, and mushroom,
- 2 tablespoons olive oil,
- 1/4 teaspoon garlic powder, and
- Salt and pepper to taste.

Preparation: **Preparation time**: 10 minutes

- Over medium heat, warm the olive oil in a large skillet.
- While stirring periodically, sauté the bell pepper, onion, and mushrooms for 5 minutes.
- Cook for a further 5 minutes, stirring regularly, after adding the eggs, garlic powder, salt, and pepper.
- In a bowl, dish up, and savor.

Peanut Butter Banana Toast

Ingredients: **Prep time**: 5 minutes

- 2 slices of whole grain bread,
- 2 teaspoons of peanut butter,
- 1/2 ripe banana, and
- 2 tablespoons of sliced almonds

Preparation: **Preparation time**: 5 minutes

- The two pieces of bread should be spread with peanut butter before being topped with banana slices and almonds.
- Toast till gently browned in a pan or toaster. Enjoy.

Baked Oatmeal

Ingredients: **Prep time**: 10 minutes

- 1 cup rolled oats,
- 1/4 tsp baking powder,
- 1/2 tsp cinnamon,
- 1/4 tsp salt,
- 1/2 cup milk,
- 1 big egg,
- 1/2 cup fresh or frozen berries,
- 2 tsp honey.

Preparation: **Preparation time**: 30 minutes

- Set the oven to 350 degrees.
- Combine the oats, baking soda, cinnamon, and salt in a large basin.
- Mix the milk, egg, and honey in another bowl.
- Combine the dry ingredients with the liquid components after adding them.
- Add the berries and stir.
- In a greased baking dish, pour the mixture and bake for 25 to 30 minutes, or until golden brown. Enjoy.

Chocolate Peanut Butter Smoothie

Ingredients: **Prep time**: 5 minutes

- ½ cup of plain Greek yogurt,
- ½ a cup of milk, two teaspoons of peanut butter,
- 1 tablespoon of chocolate powder,
- 1 teaspoon of honey, and half a frozen banana.

Preparation: **Preparation time**: 2 minutes

- Blend all of the ingredients in a blender until they are completely smooth to prepare. Enjoy.

Savory Oatmeal Bowl

Ingredients: **Prep time**: 10 minutes

- 1 cup rolled oats,
- 2 tablespoons olive oil,
- 1/4 cup chopped onion,
- 1/4 cup sliced mushrooms,
- 1/4 teaspoon smoky paprika, salt, and pepper to taste

Preparation: **Preparation time**: 10 minutes

- Over medium heat, warm the olive oil in a large skillet.
- While cooking the onion and mushrooms for 5 minutes, stirring periodically.
- Oats, smoked paprika, garlic powder, salt, and pepper are added.
- Cook for an additional 5 minutes while stirring periodically.

- In a bowl, dish up, and savor.

Breakfast burrito

Ingredients: **Prep time**: 10 minutes

- 2 big eggs,
- 2 teaspoons each of chopped bell pepper and onion,
- 2 tablespoons each of shredded cheese and salsa, and
- 2 whole wheat tortillas

Preparation: **Preparation time**: 10 minutes

- An enormous skillet should be preheated over medium heat. While cooking the onion and bell pepper for 5 minutes, stirring periodically.
- Stirring periodically, and cook the eggs for a further 5 minutes.
- Each tortilla should include cheese, salsa, bell pepper, onion, and eggs in the middle.
- Enjoy the tortillas rolled up.

Egg and Avocado Toast

Ingredients: **Prep time**: 10 minutes

- 1 tablespoon of extra virgin olive oil,
- 2 pieces of whole grain bread,
- 1/2 a ripe avocado, and
- 2 big eggs.

Preparation: **Preparation time**: 5 minutes

- Over medium heat, warm the olive oil in a large skillet.

- Add the eggs and cook for 3 to 4 minutes, depending on how done you want your eggs.

- Add salt and pepper to the eggs before placing them on top of the pieces of avocado.

- Spread the avocado and egg mixture on top of the gently browned toast. Enjoy.

A parfait of yogurt and granola

Ingredients: **Prep time**: 5 minutes

- 1/4 cup granola,

- 1/2 cup plain Greek yogurt, and

- 1/4 cup fresh fruit.

Preparation: **Preparation time**: 2 minutes

- Greek yogurt, granola, and fresh fruit should be arranged in a parfait glass. Enjoy.

Protein pancakes

Ingredients: **Prep time**: 10 minutes

- 1/2 cup rolled oats,

- 1/2 cup plain Greek yogurt,

- 2 big eggs,

- 1/2 teaspoon baking powder,

- 1/2 teaspoon cinnamon, and a dash of salt.

Preparation: **Preparation time**: 10 minutes

- In a blender, combine the oats, yogurt, eggs, baking soda, cinnamon, and salt.

- Blend until combined and smooth.

- Spray cooking spray into a big skillet and heat over medium heat.

- 1/4 cup of the batter should be added to the pan, and it should be cooked for 3–4 minutes, or until golden brown.

- Cook for another 3–4 minutes after flipping. Continue by using the remaining batter. Enjoy.

Turkey Bacon and Egg Wraps

Ingredients: **Prep time**: 10 minutes

- 2 big eggs,

- 2 pieces of turkey bacon,

- 2 whole wheat tortillas,

- 2 teaspoons of salsa, and

- 2 tablespoons of shredded cheese,

Preparation: **Preparation time**: 10 minutes

- A big skillet should be heated at medium.

- Cook the turkey bacon for 5 minutes after adding it.

- Stirring periodically, and cook the eggs for a further 5 minutes.

- Each tortilla should include eggs, bacon, cheese, and salsa in the middle. Enjoy the tortillas rolled up.

Banana Nut Oatmeal

Ingredients: **Prep time**: 10 minutes

- 1 cup rolled oats,
- 1/2 teaspoon cinnamon,
- 1/4 teaspoon salt,
- 1 cup milk,
- 1 large egg,
- 1/2 of a ripe banana,
- 2 tablespoons chopped walnuts.

Preparation: **Preparation time**: 30 minutes

- Combine the salt, cinnamon, and oats in a large basin.
- The milk and egg should be whisked together in a separate dish.
- Combine the dry ingredients with the liquid components after adding them.
- Add the walnuts and banana and stir.
- In a greased baking dish, pour the mixture and bake for 25 to 30 minutes, or until golden brown. Enjoy.

Egg and Veggie Muffins

Ingredients: **Prep time**: 10 minutes

- 2 large eggs,
- 1/4 cup diced bell pepper,
- 1/4 cup diced onion,
- 1/4 cup diced mushrooms,

- 1/4 teaspoon garlic powder,
- 1/4 teaspoon smoked paprika, salt, and pepper to taste.

Preparation: **Preparation time**: 20 minutes

- Set the oven to 350 degrees.
- Spray cooking oil in a muffin pan.
- Combine the bell pepper, onion, mushrooms, garlic powder, smoked paprika, salt, and pepper in a large bowl.
- In the muffin pans, distribute the mixture evenly.
- Every muffin cup should have one egg in it.
- Bake the eggs for 15-20 minutes, or until they are cooked to your liking. Enjoy.

Apple Cinnamon Oatmeal

Ingredients: **Prep time**: 10 minutes

- 1 cup rolled oats,
- 1/2 teaspoon cinnamon,
- 1/4 teaspoon salt,
- 1 cup milk,
- 1 big egg,
- 1/2 a ripe apple, and
- 2 tablespoons raisins.

Preparation: **Preparation time**: 30 minutes

- Combine the salt, cinnamon, and oats in a large basin.

- The milk and egg should be whisked together in a separate dish.
- Combine the dry ingredients with the liquid components after adding them.
- Add the apple and raisins and stir.
- In a greased baking dish, pour the mixture and bake for 25 to 30 minutes, or until golden brown. Enjoy.

Ham and Cheese Sandwich

Ingredients: **Prep time**: 10 minutes

- 2 slices of whole grain bread,
- 2 slices of low-fat cheese,
- 2 tablespoons of diced ham,
- 1 tablespoon olive oil.

Preparation:

- Over medium heat, warm the olive oil in a large skillet.
- For two to three minutes, while stirring periodically, add the ham.
- Sandwich cheese and ham between2 pieces of bread.
- Toast until the cheese is melted in a toaster or a pan. Enjoy.

Fruit & Nut Smoothie

Ingredients: **Prep time**: 5 minutes

- ½ cup of plain Greek -yogurt,
- ½ cup of milk, two teaspoons of chopped walnuts,
- ½ ripe banana, four cups of fresh or frozen berries, and

- 1 teaspoon of honey.

Preparation: **Preparation time**: 2 minutes

- Blend all of the ingredients in a blender until they are completely smooth to prepare. Enjoy.

Egg and Spinach Sandwich

Ingredients: **Prep time**: 10 minutes

- 2 pieces of whole grain bread,
- 2 big eggs,
- ¼ cup of spinach that has been chopped,
- 2 teaspoons of feta cheese, and
- 1 tablespoon of olive oil.

Preparation: **Preparation time**: 5 minutes

- Over medium heat, warm the olive oil in a large skillet.
- Add the eggs and cook for 3 to 4 minutes, depending on how done you want your eggs.
- Sandwich the eggs, spinach, and feta cheese between the two pieces of bread.
- Toast until the cheese is melted in a toaster or a pan. Enjoy.

LUNCH RECIPES

Quinoa-Veggie Salad

Ingredients: **Prep time**: 10 minutes

- 1 cup cooked quinoa,
- 1 cup finely chopped veggies (such as tomatoes, cucumbers, peppers, and/or onions),
- 1 tablespoon extra virgin olive oil,
- 2 tablespoons freshly squeezed lemon juice, salt, and pepper to taste.

Preparation: **Preparation time**: 2 minutes

- Quinoa, veggies, olive oil, and lemon juice should all be combined in a dish.
- Add salt and pepper to taste.
- Serving suggestions: Cool or room temperature.

Avocado-Lentil Wrap

Ingredients: **Prep time**: 10 minutes

- 2 whole wheat wraps,
- 1/4 cup cooked lentils,
- 1/2 avocado,
- 1/4 cup diced tomatoes,
- 1/4 cup diced cucumber,
- 2 teaspoons chopped red onion,
- 2 tablespoons shredded cheese,
- 2 tablespoons fresh cilantro, and salt and pepper to taste.

Preparation: **Preparation time**: 2 minutes

- Wraps should be laid down flat.
- For each wrap, first put lentils on it, then avocado, tomatoes, cucumber, red onion, cheese, and cilantro.
- Add salt and pepper to taste. Serve the wraps rolled up.

Broccoli-Cauliflower Salad

Ingredients: **Prep time**: 10 minutes

- 1 head each of broccoli and cauliflower,
- 1/4 cup each of chopped red onion, celery, and carrots,
- 2 tablespoons each of olive oil and freshly squeezed lemon juice, as well as salt and pepper to taste.

Preparation: **Preparation time**: 2 minutes

- Cut the broccoli and cauliflower into tiny florets before cooking.
- Broccoli, cauliflower, red onion, celery, carrots, olive oil, and lemon juice should all be combined in a bowl.
- Add salt and pepper to taste.
- Serving suggestions: Cool or room temperature.

Zucchini Noodles with Avocado Pesto

Ingredients: **Prep time**: 10 minutes

- 2 zucchini,
- 1 avocado,
- 14 cups fresh basil,
- 2 tablespoons extra virgin olive oil,
- 2 teaspoons freshly squeezed lemon juice, and salt and pepper to taste.

Preparation: **Preparation time**: 5 minutes

- Prepare the zucchini noodles by spiralizing them with a spiralizer.
- Combine avocado, basil, olive oil, and lemon juice in a food processor. Until smooth, process.
- Combine the pesto with the zoodles.

- Add salt and pepper to taste. Offer cold.

Sweet Potato and Black Bean Burrito

Ingredients: **Prep time**: 10 minutes

- 2 whole wheat tortillas,
- 1/2 cup cooked sweet potato,
- 1/4 cup cooked black beans,
- 1/4 cup chopped tomatoes,
- 1/4 cup diced onions,
- 2 teaspoons diced jalapeño peppers,
- 2 tablespoons shredded cheese, and salt and pepper to taste

Preparation: **Preparation time**: 5 minutes

- Lay the wraps down on a level surface to prepare.
- Each wrap should be topped with sweet potato, black beans, cheese, onions, and jalapenos.
- Add salt and pepper to taste. Serve the wraps rolled up.

Spinach-Mushroom Salad

Ingredients: **Prep time**: 10 minutes

- 2 cups spinach,
- 5 cups sliced mushrooms,
- 4 cups diced red onion,
- 4 cups diced bell pepper,
- 2 tablespoons olive oil,

- 2 tablespoons freshly squeezed lemon juice, salt, and pepper to taste.

Preparation: **Preparation time**: 2 minutes

- Spinach, mushrooms, red onion, and bell pepper should all be combined in a bowl.
- Lemon juice and olive oil should be drizzled over.
- Add salt and pepper to taste.
- Serving suggestions: Cool or room temperature.

Kale-Avocado Salad

Ingredients: **Prep time**: 10 minutes

- 2 cups chopped kale,
- 1/2 avocado,
- 1/4 cup diced tomatoes,
- 1/4 cup diced cucumber,
- 2 teaspoons diced red onion, and
- 2 tablespoons freshly squeezed lemon juice.
- To taste, salt and pepper are added.

Preparation: **Preparation time**: 2 minutes

- Kale, avocado, tomatoes, cucumber, and red onion should all be combined in a bowl.
- Add a lemon juice drizzle.
- Add salt and pepper to taste.
- Serving suggestions: Cool or room temperature.

Chickpea-Quinoa Bowl

Ingredients: **Prep time**: 10 minutes

- 1 cup cooked quinoa,
- 1/2 cup cooked chickpeas,
- 1/4 cup diced tomatoes,
- 1/4 cup diced cucumber,
- 2 teaspoons chopped red onion,
- 2 tablespoons shredded cheese, and
- 2 tablespoons fresh parsley are the ingredients.
- To taste, salt and pepper are added.

Preparation: **Preparation time**: 2 minutes

- Quinoa, chickpeas, tomatoes, cucumber, red onion, cheese, and parsley should all be combined in a dish.
- Add salt and pepper to taste.
- Serving suggestions: Cool or room temperature.

Lentil-Brown Rice Bowl

Ingredients: **Prep time**: 10 minutes

- 2 teaspoons chopped red onion,
- 2 tablespoons freshly squeezed lemon juice,
- 1/2 cup cooked brown rice,
- 1/2 cup cooked lentils,
- 1/4 cup diced tomatoes,
- 1/4 cup diced cucumber, salt and pepper to taste.

Preparation: **Preparation time:** 2 minutes

- Brown rice, lentils, tomatoes, cucumber, and red onion should all be combined in a dish.
- Add a lemon juice drizzle.
- Add salt and pepper to taste.
- Serving suggestions: Cool or room temperature.

Broccoli-Carrot Salad

Ingredients: **Prep time:** 10 minutes

- 2 cups chopped broccoli,
- 1/2 cup grated carrots,
- 1/4 cup diced red onion,
- 1/4 cup diced celery,
- 2 teaspoons of olive oil,
- 2 tablespoons of freshly squeezed lemon juice, and salt and pepper to taste.

Preparation: **Preparation time:** 2 minutes

- Broccoli, carrots, red onion, and celery should all be combined in a bowl.
- Lemon juice and olive oil should be drizzled over.
- Add salt and pepper to taste.
- Serving suggestions: Cool or room temperature.

Cucumber-Tomato Salad

Ingredients: **Prep time**: 10 minutes

- 2 cups diced cucumber,

- 1/2 cup diced tomatoes,

- 1/4 cup chopped red onion,

- 1/4 cup diced bell pepper,

- 2 teaspoons of olive oil,

- 2 tablespoons of freshly squeezed lemon juice, and salt and pepper to taste.

Preparation: **Preparation time**: 2 minutes

- Cucumber, tomatoes, red onion, and bell pepper should all be combined in a bowl.

- Lemon juice and olive oil should be drizzled over.

- Add salt and pepper to taste.

- Serving suggestions: Cool or room temperature.

Eggplant-Quinoa Bowl

Ingredients: **Prep time**: 10 minutes

- 2 tablespoons sliced jalapeño peppers,

- 2 tablespoons freshly squeezed lemon juice,

- 1 cup cooked quinoa,

- 1/2 cup diced eggplant,

- 1/4 cup diced tomatoes,

- 1/4 cup diced onions, and salt and pepper to taste

Preparation: 　　　　　　　　**Preparation time**: 5 minutes

- Quinoa, eggplant, tomatoes, onions, and jalapeño peppers should all be combined in a bowl.
- Add a lemon juice drizzle.
- Add salt and pepper to taste.
- Serving suggestions: Cool or room temperature.

Chickpea-Kale Salad

Ingredients: 　　　　　　　**Prep time**: 10 minutes

- 2 cups chopped kale,
- 1/2 cup cooked chickpeas,
- 1/4 cup diced tomatoes,
- 1/4 cup diced cucumber,
- 2 tablespoons diced red onion,
- 2 teaspoons extra virgin olive oil,
- 2 tablespoons freshly squeezed lemon juice, salt, and pepper to taste.

Preparation: 　　　　　　　**Preparation time**: 5 minutes

- Kale, chickpeas, tomatoes, cucumber, and red onion should all be combined in a dish.
- Lemon juice and olive oil should be drizzled over.
- Add salt and pepper to taste.
- Serving suggestions: Cool or room temperature.

Sweet Potato-Black Bean Burrito

Ingredients: **Prep time**: 10 minutes**:**

- 2 whole wheat tortillas,
- 1/2 cup cooked sweet potato,
- 1/4 cup cooked black beans,
- 1/4 cup chopped tomatoes,
- 1/4 cup diced onions,
- 2 teaspoons diced jalapeño peppers,
- 2 tablespoons shredded cheese, and salt and pepper to taste

Preparation: **Preparation time**: 5 minutes

- Lay the wraps down on a level surface to prepare.
- Each wrap should be topped with sweet potato, black beans, cheese, onions, and jalapenos.
- Add some salt and pepper to it. Serve the wraps rolled up.

Roasted Vegetable Bowl

Ingredients: **Prep time**: 10 minutes

- 2 teaspoons olive oil,
- 2 tablespoons freshly squeezed lemon juice, salt, and pepper to taste,
- 1 cup chopped veggies of your choosing (such as tomatoes, peppers, and/or onions).

Preparation: **Preparation time**: 15 minutes

- The oven should be heated to 350°F (175°C).

- Vegetables are spread out on a baking pan.

- Lemon juice and olive oil should be drizzled over.

- Add salt and pepper to taste.

- Vegetables should be tender after 15 minutes under the broiler.

- Dish out in a bowl.

Farro-Veggie Bowl

Ingredients: **Prep time**: 10 minutes

- 2 teaspoons olive oil,

- 2 tablespoons freshly squeezed lemon juice, salt, and pepper to taste,

- 1 cup cooked farro,

- 1 cup chopped veggies of your choosing (such as tomatoes, peppers, and/or onions).

Preparation: **Preparation time**: 2 minutes

- Farro, veggies, olive oil, and lemon juice should all be combined in a bowl.

- Add salt and pepper to taste.

- Serving suggestions: Cool or room temperature.

Cauliflower-Kale Bowl

Ingredients: **Prep time**: 10 minutes

- 1 cup cooked cauliflower,

- 1 cup chopped kale,

- 1/4 cup diced tomatoes,

- 1/4 cup diced cucumber,
- 2 tablespoons red onion.
- 2 tablespoons olive oil,
- 2 tablespoons freshly squeezed lemon juice, salt, and pepper to taste.

Preparation: **Preparation time**: 5 minutes

- Cauliflower, kale, tomatoes, cucumber, and red onion should all be combined in a bowl.
- Lemon juice and olive oil should be drizzled over.
- Add salt and pepper to taste.
- Serving suggestions: Cool or room temperature.

Avocado-Spinach Salad

Ingredients: **Prep time**: 10 minutes

- 2 cups spinach,
- 1/2 avocado,
- 1/4 cup diced tomatoes,
- 1/4 cup diced cucumber,
- 2 tablespoons sliced red onion, and salt and pepper to taste.

Preparation: **Preparation time**: 5 minutes

- Spinach, avocado, tomatoes, cucumber, and red onion should all be combined in a bowl.
- Add a lemon juice drizzle.
- Add salt and pepper to taste.

- Serving suggestions: Cool or room temperature.

Quinoa-Mushroom Bowl

Ingredients: **Prep time**: 10 minutes

- 1 cup cooked quinoa,

- half a cup of sliced mushrooms,

- 1/4 cup diced tomatoes,

- 1/4 cup diced onions,

- 2 teaspoons chopped jalapeño peppers,

- 2 tablespoons shredded cheese,

- 2 tablespoons fresh parsley, and salt and pepper to taste.

Preparation: **Preparation time**: 5 minutes

- Quinoa, mushrooms, tomatoes, onions, jalapeño peppers, cheese, and parsley should be combined in a dish.

- Add salt and pepper to taste.

- Serving suggestions: Cool or room temperature.

Roasted butternut squash salad

Ingredients: **Prep time**: 10 minutes

- 1 cup cubed squash,

- 1/4 cup chopped red onion,

- 1/4 cup diced bell pepper,

- 2 teaspoons olive oil,

- 2 tablespoons freshly squeezed lemon juice, salt, and pepper to taste.

Preparation:

- The oven should be heated to 350°F (175°C).

- On a baking pan, spread out the butternut squash.

- Lemon juice and olive oil should be drizzled over.

- Add salt and pepper to taste. Vegetables should be tender after 15 minutes under the broiler.

- Combine bell pepper, red onion, and butternut squash in a bowl.

- Serving suggestions: Cool or room temperature.

DINNER RECIPES

Stir-fried kale, quinoa, and asparagus

Ingredients:

Prep time: 10 minutes

- 2 cups cooked quinoa,
- 2 cups kale,
- 2 cups asparagus,
- 2 tablespoons extra virgin olive oil,

- 1 tablespoon minced garlic, and
- 1 teaspoon salt

Preparation: **Preparation time**: 10 minutes

- In a big skillet, heat the olive oil over medium heat, then add the garlic.
- Add the asparagus and salt once the garlic begins to smell good, and simmer for three minutes.
- Kale and quinoa should then be added and cooked for an additional 5 minutes.

Cauliflower Mac and Cheese

Ingredients: **Prep time**: 5 minutes

- 1 head of cauliflower,
- 1 cup of low-fat milk,
- 2 tablespoons of butter,
- 2 tablespoons of all-purpose flour,
- 1 cup of shredded cheddar cheese,
- 1 teaspoon of crushed mustard, and
- 1 teaspoon of salt.

Preparation: **Preparation time**: 10 minutes

- Smallen the cauliflower florets, then steam for 8 minutes.
- Dissolve the spread in a medium pot over medium intensity, then rush in the flour until consolidated.

- As it begins to thicken, mix in the milk, mustard, and salt.
- When everything is combined, add the cheese and stir until it melts.

Broccoli and Zucchini Fritters

Ingredients: **Prep time**: 10 minutes

- 1 head of broccoli,
- 1 zucchini,
- 2 eggs,
- 2 tablespoons of all-purpose flour,
- 1 teaspoon each of garlic powder, onion powder, and salt.

Preparation: **Preparation time**: 10 minutes

- Combine the grated broccoli and zucchini in a bowl.
- Eggs, flour, garlic powder, onion powder, and salt should all be combined in different bowls.
- Mix the veggies with the egg mixture after adding them.
- Spoonfuls of the mixture should be dropped into a hot, big pan over medium heat.
- Cook for 3 to 4 minutes on each side or until golden brown.

Spinach and Feta Frittata

Ingredients: **Prep time**: 10 minutes

- eggs,
- 1/4 cup milk,

- 2 cups spinach,
- 1/2 cup feta cheese,
- 2 tablespoons olive oil,
- 1 teaspoon garlic powder, and
- 1 teaspoon salt.

Preparation: **Preparation time**: 10 minutes

- In a big skillet over medium heat, warm the olive oil.
- For three minutes, until the spinach has wilted, add the garlic powder and spinach.
- Whisk the eggs and milk together in another basin.
- When the edges are set, add the egg mixture to the spinach and simmer for 3 minutes.
- Cook for three more minutes after adding the feta cheese.
- Serve after adding salt to taste.

Avocado and egg toast

Ingredients: **Prep time**: 5 minutes

- 2 pieces of whole wheat bread,
- 1 avocado,
- 2 eggs,
- 1 teaspoon of olive oil, and
- 1 teaspoon of salt.

Preparation: **Preparation time**: 5 minutes

- Over medium heat, warm the olive oil in a large skillet.
- When the whites are set, crack the eggs into the pan and cook for 3 minutes.
- Toast the bread, then spread the avocado on it.
- Salt the eggs and then place them on top of the bread.

Roasted Brussels Sprouts Salad

Ingredients: **Prep time**: 10 minutes

- 1 pound of Brussels sprouts,
- 2 tablespoons of olive oil,
- 1 teaspoon each of garlic powder, onion powder, and salt,
- 1/2 cup each of walnuts and dried cranberries.
- 2 teaspoons of balsamic vinegar.

Preparation: **Preparation time**: 15 minutes

- Set the oven to 400°F.
- Place the Brussels sprouts on a baking sheet after cutting them in half.
- Olive oil should be drizzled over the dish before salt, garlic powder, and onion powder are added. Golden brown after 15 minutes of roasting.
- The Brussels sprouts, walnuts, cranberries, and balsamic vinegar should all be put in a big bowl and stirred well.

Garlic and Herb Roasted Salmon

Ingredients: **Prep time**: 5 minutes

- 2 salmon fillets,
- 2 tablespoons of extra virgin olive oil,
- 1 teaspoon each of garlic powder, dried oregano, dried parsley, and salt.

Preparation: **Preparation time**: 15 minutes

- Set the oven to 400 degrees Fahrenheit.
- Olive oil should be used after placing the salmon on a baking pan.
- Salt, oregano, parsley, and garlic powder should be added on top.
- Cook the fish thoroughly in the oven for 12 to 15 minutes.

Zucchini Noodle Bowl

Ingredients: **Prep time**: 10 minutes

- 2 zucchinis,
- 2 tablespoons olive oil,
- 1 teaspoon each of garlic powder, onion powder, and salt,
- 1/2 cup each of cherry tomatoes, black beans, corn, and lemon juice.

Preparation: **Preparation time**: 8 minutes

- To create zucchini noodles, use a spiralizer or a julienne peeler.

- Garlic and onion powder are added to the olive oil while it is heating in a large pan over medium heat.
- Salt the zucchini noodles and then incorporate them.
- Noodles should be softened after 5 minutes of cooking.
- Lastly, blend the tomatoes, black beans, corn, and lemon juice by adding them all together and stirring.

Lentil Soup

Ingredients: **Prep time**: 10 minutes

- 1 cup lentils,
- 2 cups vegetable broth,
- 1 carrot,
- 2 cloves of garlic,
- 1 teaspoon cumin, and
- 1 teaspoon salt.

Preparation: **Preparation time**: 25 minutes

- An enormous pot should be heated to medium heat before the onion, carrot, and garlic are added.
- To soften the veggies, cook for 5 minutes. Bring to a boil after adding the lentils, vegetable broth, cumin, and salt.
- Once the lentils are fully cooked, reduce the heat to low and let the mixture simmer for 20 minutes.

Cucumber Quinoa Salad

Ingredients: **Prep time**: 10 minutes

- 1 cup cooked quinoa,
- 1 cucumber,
- 2 teaspoons olive oil,
- 2 tablespoons lemon juice,
- 1 teaspoon garlic powder, and
- 1 teaspoon dried oregano.

. .

Preparation: **Preparation time**: 5 minutes

- Quinoa, cucumber, tomatoes, and feta cheese should all be mixed in a big dish.
- Mix the olive oil, lemon juice, garlic powder, and oregano in another bowl.
- After adding the dressing to the salad, toss everything together.

Kale salad with apples and walnuts

Ingredients: **Prep time**: 10 minutes

- 2 cups of kale,
- 1 apple,
- 1/2 cup of walnuts,
- 2 tablespoons each of apple cider vinegar and olive oil,
- 1 teaspoon each of garlic powder and salt.

.

Preparation: **Preparation time**: 5 minutes

- Place the kale in a big bowl once it has been cut into thin pieces.
- Slice the apple thinly after coring it.
- Stir together the apple slices and walnuts in the bowl after adding them.
- Combine the olive oil, apple cider vinegar, salt, garlic powder, and pepper in another bowl.
- After adding the dressing to the salad, toss everything together.

Lentil and Quinoa Veggie Burgers

Ingredients: **Prep time**: 10 minutes

- 1 cup cooked lentils,
- 1 cup cooked quinoa,
- 1/4 cup chopped onions,
- 1/4 cup diced bell peppers,
- 2 tablespoons flaxseed meal,
- 2 tablespoons olive oil,
- 1 teaspoon garlic powder, and
- 1 teaspoon cumin.

Preparation: **Preparation time**: 10 minutes

- In a large bowl, add the lentils, quinoa, onions, bell peppers, flaxseed meal, olive oil, garlic powder, and cumin.
- Mix well. Patties made from the mixture should be heated in a big pan over medium heat.

- The patties should be added to the pan and cooked for 3–4 minutes until golden brown on each side.

Lentil and Kale Quinoa Bowl

Ingredients: **Prep time**: 10 minutes

- 1 cup cooked quinoa,
- 1 cup cooked lentils,
- 2 cups of kale,
- 2 tablespoons of extra virgin olive oil,
- 1 teaspoon each of garlic powder, cumin, and salt.

Preparation: **Preparation time**: 10 minutes

- Garlic, cumin, and salt are added to the olive oil while it is heating up in a large pan over medium heat.
- After adding, simmer the kale for 3 minutes, or until wilted.
- Lentils and quinoa are added, and the cooking time is increased by 5 minutes. In a bowl, dish up, and savor.

Cauliflower Fried Rice

Ingredients: **Prep time**: 10 minutes

- 1 head of cauliflower,
- 2 eggs,
- 2 tablespoons of extra-virgin olive oil,
- 1 teaspoon each of garlic powder, onion powder, and salt.

Preparation: **Preparation time**: 8 minutes

- Cutting the cauliflower into tiny florets, prepare it by pulsing it in a food processor until it resembles rice.
- Garlic and onion powder are added to the olive oil while it is heating in a large pan over medium heat.
- Salt the cauliflower "rice" before adding it. Cook the cauliflower for 5 minutes, or until it softens.
- Crack the eggs on the other side of the pan from where the cauliflower is pushed to one side.
- Combine the cauliflower with the scrambled eggs when they have finished cooking.

Baked Sweet Potato and Chickpea Fries

Ingredients: **Prep time**: 10 minutes

- 2 big sweet potatoes,
- 1 can of chickpeas,
- 2 tablespoons of extra virgin olive oil,
- 1 teaspoon each of smoked paprika, onion powder, garlic powder, and salt.

Preparation: **Preparation time**: 25 minutes

- Set the oven's temperature to 425 F.
- Sweet potatoes should be cut into fries and put on a baking pan.
- Add the chickpeas to the baking sheet after draining and rinsing them.

- Add salt, smoked paprika, garlic powder, onion powder, and olive oil after drizzling.
- Bake the fries for 25 minutes, or until they are crisp and golden.

Mushroom and Spinach Quiche

Ingredients: **Prep time**: 10 minutes

- 2 cups spinach,
- 1 cup mushrooms,
- 2 eggs,
- 1/2 cup milk,
- 2 tablespoons olive oil,
- 1 teaspoon garlic powder,
- 1 teaspoon salt, and
- 1 frozen pie crust.

Preparation: **Preparation time**: 30 minutes

- Set the broiler to 400 degrees Fahrenheit.
- In an enormous skillet set over medium intensity, add the olive oil and garlic.
- Add the mushrooms and spinach when the garlic has begun to smell good, and simmer for 3 minutes, or until the mushrooms are tender.
- Whisk together the eggs, milk, and salt in a separate bowl.
- Place the spinach and mushroom mixture on top of the egg mixture in the pie shell.

- Bake the quiche for 25 minutes, or until golden brown.

Salmon and Veggie Stir-Fry

Ingredients: **Prep time**: 10 minutes

- 2 salmon filets,
- 2 cups broccoli,
- 2 cups bell peppers,
- 2 tablespoons olive oil,
- 1 teaspoon each of garlic powder, onion powder, and salt.

Preparation: **Preparation time**: 10 minutes

- Salmon should be cubed into tiny pieces and kept aside.
- Garlic and onion powder are added to the olive oil while it is heating in a large pan over medium heat.
- Add salt and then the broccoli and bell peppers.
- To soften the veggies, cook for 5 minutes.
- Once the salmon is fully cooked, add the salmon cubes and cook for an additional 3–4 minutes.

Baked Eggplant Parmesan

Ingredients: **Prep time**: 10 minutes

- 1 eggplant,
- 2 eggs,
- 2 tablespoons of all-purpose flour,
- 1 cup breadcrumbs,

- 1 teaspoon each of garlic powder, onion powder, and salt, and 1/2 cup shredded mozzarella cheese.

Preparation: **Preparation time**: 20 minutes

- Set the oven to 375 degrees Fahrenheit.
- Slice the eggplant thinly, then put it aside.
- The eggs should be whisked together in a small bowl.
- Combine the flour, breadcrumbs, salt, garlic powder, and onion powder in a separate shallow basin.
- Slices of eggplant should be dipped into the egg mixture first, followed by the breadcrumb mixture.
- On a baking sheet, arrange the eggplant slices and top with mozzarella cheese.
- The eggplant must be baked for 20 minutes or until golden brown.

Grilled Veggie skewers

Ingredients: **Prep time**: 10 minutes

- 1 red onion,
- 1 red bell pepper,
- 1 yellow bell pepper,
- 1 zucchini,
- 2 tablespoons of extra virgin olive oil,
- 1 teaspoon each of garlic powder, onion powder, smoky paprika, and salt.

Preparation: **Preparation time**: 5 minutes

- On skewers, arrange the cubed zucchini, bell peppers, and onion.
- Garlic and onion powder are added to the olive oil while it is heating in a large pan over medium heat.
- Salt and smoked paprika are added to the pan along with the skewers.
- To soften the veggies, cook for 5 minutes.

Baked Apple Oatmeal

Ingredients: **Prep time**: 10 minutes

- 2 apples,
- 2 cups rolled oats,
- 2 cups almond milk,
- 2 tablespoons maple syrup,
- 1 teaspoon cinnamon, and
- 1 teaspoon salt are the ingredients.

Preparation: **Preparation time**: 25 minutes

- Set the oven to 375 degrees Fahrenheit.
- Apples should be cored and sliced thinly.
- Put the apple slices and rolled oats on a dish that can go in the oven.

- Add the salt, cinnamon, and maple syrup after pouring the almond milk over the oats.
- The oats must be baked for 25 minutes to get golden brown.

DESSERT RECIPES

Low-carb coconut flour pancakes

Ingredients: **Prep time**: 10 minutes

- 2 eggs
- 1/4 cup of coconut flour
- 1/4 teaspoon baking pop
- 2 tablespoons liquefied coconut oil
- Salt,
- 1/4 teaspoon
- 1/4 cup almond milk, unsweetened
- 2 teaspoons of honey

Preparation: **Preparation time**: 5 minutes

- Coconut flour, eggs, coconut oil, baking soda, and salt should all be mixed in a bowl during preparation.
- Add honey and almond milk and stir.
- An oil-coated skillet is heated at medium-high heat.
- When the batter is ready, drop 1/4 cup into the pan and cook for 3 minutes on each side, or until golden brown.
- Serve with your preferred garnishes.

Low-carbs peanut butter cookies

Ingredients: **Prep time**: 10 minutes

- 1 tablespoon creamy peanut butter

- 1/4 teaspoon baking soda
- 3 tablespoons of honey
- 1 egg
- 1/4 teaspoon salt

Preparation: **Preparation time**: 10 minutes

- Prepare the ingredients by combining the peanut butter, honey, baking soda, and salt in a bowl.
- When everything is blended, add the egg.
- Drop the dough onto a baking sheet that has been buttered using a cookie scoop or spoon.
- Bake the cookies at 350°F for 8 to 10 minutes, or until golden brown.
- Before serving, allow the cookies to cool.

Low-carb chocolate chip muffins

Ingredients: **Prep time**: 10 minutes

- 1/4 cup of coconut flour
- 1/2 cup of almond flour
- Baking soda,
- 1 teaspoon salt,
- 1/4 teaspoon chocolate chunks
- 2 eggs
- 1/2 cup sugar,
- 1/4 cup honey,
- 1/4 cup melted coconut oil, and

- 1 teaspoon vanilla extract.

Preparation: **Preparation time**: 20 minutes

- Prepare the ingredients by combining the baking soda, salt, coconut flour, and almond flour in a bowl.
- Whisk the eggs, coconut oil, honey, and vanilla extract in another dish.
- Mix all of the components together after adding the wet ones to the dry ones.
- Add the chocolate chunks and stir.
- Divide the batter among the muffin cups in a muffin tray that has been greased with coconut oil.
- A toothpick put into the middle of the muffin should come out clean after 18 to 20 minutes of baking at 350°F.
- Prior to serving, let the muffins cool.

Low-carbs lemon Poppyseed Cake

Ingredients: **Prep time**: 10 minutes

- 1 teaspoon baking powder
- 1/2 cup almond flour
- 1/4 cup coconut flour
- salt,
- 1/4 teaspoon
- 2 eggs
- 1/4 cup coconut oil that has melted
- 2 tablespoons lemon juice

- 1/4 cup honey

- 2 tablespoons poppy seeds

- 1 teaspoon vanilla concentrate

Preparation: **Preparation time**: 25 minutes

- Almond flour, coconut flour, baking powder, and salt should all be incorporated into a bowl for preparation.

- The eggs, coconut oil, honey, lemon juice, and vanilla essence should all be combined in a separate bowl.

- Mix all of the components together after adding the wet ones to the dry ones.

- Add the poppy seeds and stir.

- Pour the batter into an 8-inch cake pan that has been greased with coconut oil.

- Until a toothpick put into the middle of the cake comes out clean, bake the cake at 350°F for 20 to 25 minutes.

- The cake should cool before being served.

Low-carbs Apple Crisp

Ingredients: **Prep time**: 10 minutes

- 4 apples, peeled, cored, and cut, are required.

- 1/4 cup coconut flour

- 1/4 teaspoon cinnamon

- 1/2 cup almond flour

- 1/8 tsp. nutmeg

- 1/4 teaspoon salt
- 1/4 cup coconut oil that has been melted
- 1/4 cup honey

Preparation: **Preparation time**: 30 minutes

- The oven should be preheated to 350 degrees.
- The apples should be put in an 8-inch baking dish.
- Combine the salt, cinnamon, nutmeg, coconut flour, and almond flour in a bowl.
- Honey and coconut oil should be blended.
- Overlay the apples with the mixture.
- Bake the topping for 25 to 30 minutes, or until golden brown.
- Serve the crisp when it has had time to cool.

Low-Carb Chocolate Mousse

Ingredients: **Prep time**: 10 minutes

- 2 pitted and peeled avocados;
- 1/4 cup cocoa powder;
- 1 teaspoon vanilla concentrate
- 1/4 cup honey.

Preparation: **Preparation time**: 2 hours

- Prepare the avocados, cocoa powder, honey, and vanilla extract in a food processor or blender.
- Blend till creamy and smooth.

- Divide the mousse among the serving bowls.
- Serve chilled at least two hours prior.

Low-Carb Raspberry Cheesecake

Ingredients: **Prep time**: 10 minutes

- 1/4 cup coconut flour
- 1/4 teaspoon baking soda
- 1/2 cup almond flour
- 1/4 teaspoon salt
- 1/4 cup coconut oil that has been melted
- 1/4 cup honey
- 2 eggs
- Softened 8 ounces of cream cheese
- 1/2 cup of raspberry preserves

Preparation: **Preparation time**: 25 minutes

- The oven should be preheated to 350 degrees.
- Almond flour, coconut flour, baking soda, and salt should be combined in a bowl.
- Combine the eggs, coconut oil, honey, and another bowl.
- Combine the dry ingredients with the liquid components after adding them.
- Use coconut oil to lube a 8-inch spring form skillet.
- In the pan, spread the batter.

- Mix the cream cheese and raspberry preserves well in another bowl. Over the batter, spoon the mixture.
- Bake the cheesecake for 20 to 25 minutes, or until a toothpick inserted in the middle comes out clean.
- Prior to serving, let the cheesecake cool.

Low-carb carrot cake

Ingredients: **Prep time**: 10 minutes

- 1 teaspoon of baking powder,
- 1/4 cup of coconut flour,
- 1/2 cup of almond flour, and
- 1/4 teaspoon salt.
- 2 eggs
- 1/4 cup of melted coconut oil
- 1/4 cup honey,
- 1 tsp. vanilla essence
- 1 cup of shredded carrots
- 1/2 cup chopped walnuts

Preparation: **Preparation time**: 25 minutes

- 350 degrees should be the prepared oven temperature.
- Salt, baking powder, almond flour, and coconut flour should all be blended in a bowl.
- In another bowl, combine the eggs, coconut oil, honey, and vanilla extract.

- After adding the wet ingredients to the dry ones, combine all the ingredients.
- Stir in the walnuts and carrots.
- Fill an 8-inch cake pan with the batter after greasing the pan with coconut oil.
- After 20 to 25 minutes of baking, a toothpick inserted into the center of the cake should come out clean.
- The cake should cool completely before serving.

Banana bread made with low carbs

Ingredients: **Prep time**: 10 minutes

- Baking soda,
- 1 teaspoon salt,
- 1/4 teaspoon
- 2 eggs,
- 1/4 cup coconut flour,
- 1/2 cup almond flour
- 1/4 cup melted coconut oil
- 14 cups of honey
- ½ cup of mashed ripe bananas
- 1 teaspoon of vanilla extract

Preparation: **Preparation time**: 25 minutes

- 350 degrees should be the prepared oven temperature.
- In a bowl, add salt, baking soda, coconut flour, and almond flour.

- In another bowl, combine the eggs, coconut oil, honey, and vanilla extract.

- After adding the wet ingredients to the dry ones, combine all the ingredients.

- Stir in the mashed banana.

- Fill an 8-inch loaf pan with the batter after greasing the pan with coconut oil.

- After 20 to 25 minutes of baking, a toothpick inserted into the center of the bread should come out clean.

- Let the bread cool before serving.

Low-carb coconut cookies

Ingredients: **Prep time**: 10 minutes

- 3 egg whites
- 1/4 teaspoon cream of tartar,
- 1/4 cup honey,
- 1/2 teaspoon vanilla essence, and
- 1/4 teaspoon almond extract are combined with
- 3/4 cup of finely chopped coconut.

Preparation: **Preparation time**: 15 minutes

- 350 degrees should be the prepared oven temperature.

- In a bowl, whisk the egg whites and cream of tartar together until stiff peaks are formed. In another dish, mix the almond, vanilla, and honey extracts.

- Fold the egg whites into the honey mixture once it has been mixed.
- Add the coconut shavings gradually. Grease a baking sheet with coconut oil.
- The batter should be poured onto the baking sheet one spoonful at a time.
- The macaroons should be baked for 10 to 12 minutes, or until just beginning to color.
- Allow the macaroons to cool before serving.

Low-carb Almond Joy Bars

Ingredients: **Prep time**: 10 minutes

- 1/4 cup coconut flour
- 1/4 teaspoon baking soda Joy Bars
- 1/4 teaspoon salt,
- 1/2 cup almond flour
- 2 eggs
- 1/4 cup melted coconut oil
- 1/2 cup coconut shreds
- 1/2 cup of chopped almonds
- 1/4 cup honey
- 1/2 cup of dark chocolate chips without added sugar

Preparation: **Preparation time**: 25 minutes

- 350 degrees should be the prepared oven temperature.
- In a bowl, add salt, baking soda, coconut flour, and almond flour.

- In another dish, combine the eggs, honey, and coconut oil.
- After adding the wet ingredients to the dry ones, combine all the ingredients.
- Add the coconut, almond, and chocolate chunks to the mixture.
- Spread the batter into a prepared 8-inch baking dish with coconut oil.
- After 20 to 25 minutes, a toothpick inserted in the center should come out clean. Let the bars cool before serving.

Low-carb chocolate truffle

Ingredients: **Prep time**: 10 minutes

- 1/4 cup cocoa powder
- 1 teaspoon vanilla extract
- 1/4 cup honey
- 1/2 cup coconut oil

Preparation: **Preparation time**: 2 hours

- To get ready, warm up the coconut oil in a saucepan over low heat.
- Add the cocoa powder, honey, and vanilla extract after blending.
- Put the ingredients in an 8-inch baking dish that has been buttered.
- Serve chilled for two hours before serving.

Low-carb chocolate chip cookies

Ingredients: **Prep time**: 10 minutes

- 1/2 cup almond flour,
- 1/2 cup sugar,

- 1 teaspoon vanilla extract,
- 1/4 cup melted coconut oil,
- 1/2 cup of salt, and
- 1/4 cup of chocolate chips that aren't.

Preparation: **Preparation time**: 10 minutes

- The baking soda, salt, coconut flour, and almond flour should be combined in a bowl to prepare the ingredients.
- In another bowl, combine the eggs, coconut oil, honey, and vanilla extract.
- After adding the wet ingredients to the dry ones, combine all the ingredients.
- Stir in the chocolate bits.
- Once the baking sheet has been prepared with coconut oil, the batter should be put into it one spoonful at a time.
- The cookies should be baked for 8 to 10 minutes, or until golden brown, at 350°F.
- Allow the cookies to cool before serving.

Low-Carb Ingredients for Pumpkin Pie

Ingredients: **Prep time**: 10 minutes

- 2 eggs,
- 1 teaspoon of baking soda,
- 1/2 teaspoon of salt,
- 1/4 cup each of coconut flour and almond flour.

- 1/4 cup of melted coconut oil
- 1/4 cup honey,
- 1 teaspoon of vanilla extract
- 1/2 cup of pumpkin puree

Preparation: **Preparation time**: 25 minutes

- 350 degrees should be the prepared oven temperature.
- Salt, baking powder, almond flour, and coconut flour should all be blended in a bowl.
- In another bowl, combine the eggs, coconut oil, honey, and vanilla extract.
- After adding the wet ingredients to the dry ones, combine all the ingredients.
- Stir in the pumpkin puree.
- Fill an 8-inch pie dish with the batter after greasing the pan with coconut oil.
- After 20 to 25 minutes of baking, a toothpick inserted into the center of the pie should come out clean.
- Let the pie cool before serving.

Low-carbs Almond Joy Cupcakes

Ingredients: **Prep time**: 10 minutes

- 1 teaspoon baking powder
- 1/2 cup almond flour
- 1/4 cup coconut flour

- 1/4 teaspoon salt,
- 2 eggs
- 1/4 cup coconut oil that has melted
- 1/2 cup coconut shreds
- 1/4 cup honey
- 1/2 cup of sliced almonds
- 1/2 cup sugar-free chips made from dark chocolate

Preparation: **Preparation time**: 20 minutes

- The oven should be preheated to 350 degrees.
- Almond flour, coconut flour, baking powder, and salt should all be combined in a bowl.
- Whisk the eggs, coconut oil, and honey in another bowl.
- Mix all of the components after adding the wet ones to the dry ones.
- Add the chocolate chunks, almond pieces, and coconut to the mixture.
- Divide the batter among the muffin cups in a 12-cup muffin pan that has been greased with coconut oil.
- Bake the cupcakes for 18 to 20 minutes, or until a toothpick inserted into the middle comes out clean.
- Before serving, allow the cupcakes to cool.

Low-carb chocolate cake

Ingredients: **Prep time**: 10 minutes

- 2 eggs,
- 1 teaspoon baking soda,

- 1/2 teaspoon salt,
- 1/4 cup each of coconut flour and almond flour.
- 1/4 cup of melted coconut oil
- 1/4 cups honey,
- 1/2 cup of cocoa powder
- 1 teaspoon of vanilla extract

Preparation: **Preparation time**: 25 minutes

- 350 degrees should be the prepared oven temperature.
- Salt, baking powder, almond flour, and coconut flour should all be blended in a bowl.
- In another bowl, combine the eggs, coconut oil, honey, and vanilla extract.
- After adding the wet ingredients to the dry ones, combine all the ingredients.
- Stir in the cocoa powder after adding it.
- Fill an 8-inch cake pan with the batter after greasing the pan with coconut oil.
- After 20 to 25 minutes of baking, a toothpick inserted into the center of the cake should come out clean.
- The cake should cool completely before serving.

Low-carbs coconut cream pie

Ingredients: **Prep time**: 10 minutes

- 1/2 cup of almond flour,

- 1/4 teaspoon of baking soda,
- 1/4 teaspoon of coconut flour
- 2 eggs
- 1/2 cup of coconut shreds
- 1 teaspoon vanilla extract
- 1/4 cup heated coconut oil
- 1/4 cup honey
- 1/2 cup coconut cream

Preparation: **Preparation time**: 25 minutes

- 350 degrees should be the prepared oven temperature.
- In a bowl, add salt, baking soda, coconut flour, and almond flour.
- In another bowl, combine the eggs, coconut oil, honey, and vanilla extract.
- After adding the wet ingredients to the dry ones, combine all the ingredients.
- Stir in the shredded coconut.
- Fill an 8-inch pie dish with the batter after greasing the pan with coconut oil.
- After 20 to 25 minutes of baking, a toothpick inserted into the center of the pie should come out clean.
- Let the pie cool before adding the coconut cream.
- Serve chilled for two hours before serving.

Low-carbs Strawberry Shortcake

Ingredients: **Prep time**: 10 minutes

- 1/2 cup of almond flour
- 1/4 cup of coconut flour.
- 1 teaspoon of salt, one teaspoon of baking soda
- 2 eggs
- 1/4 cup heated coconut oil
- 1/4 cup honey
- 1 cup sliced strawberries
- 1 teaspoon vanilla essence

Preparation: **Preparation time**: 25 minutes

- 350 degrees should be the prepared oven temperature.
- Salt, baking powder, almond flour, and coconut flour should all be blended in a bowl.
- In another bowl, combine the eggs, coconut oil, honey, and vanilla extract.
- After adding the wet ingredients to the dry ones, combine all the ingredients.
- Fill an 8-inch cake pan with the batter after greasing the pan with coconut oil.
- After 20 to 25 minutes of baking, a toothpick inserted into the center of the cake should come out clean.
- Let the cake cool before adding the strawberry pieces.

Low-carbs Chocolate Pudding

Ingredients: **Prep time**: 10 minutes

- 1/4 cup of cocoa powder
- 2 eggs and two teaspoons of cornstarch
- 1/4 cup honey
- 1 teaspoon of vanilla essence and
- 2 glasses of almond milk

Preparation: **Preparation time**: 2 hours

- In a saucepan, combine the cornstarch, honey, and cocoa powder to make the mixture.
- Whisk in the eggs after adding them. Whisk in the almond milk gently to combine.
- Cook the mixture over medium heat, stirring constantly, until it boils.
- Reduce the heat to low as the pudding thickens, then whisk constantly for 2 minutes.
- After removing the pan from the heat, add the vanilla essence.
- Separate serving dishes should be used for the pudding.
- Serve chilled for two hours before serving.

Low-carbs Tiramisu

Ingredients: **Prep time**: 10 minutes

- 2 eggs
- 1/4 cup honey,
- 1/4 teaspoon almond extract,

- 1 teaspoon vanilla extract,
- 2 tablespoons of espresso
- 1/2 cup of almond flour,
- 1/4 teaspoon of baking soda,
- 1/4 teaspoon of coconut flour
- 1/2 cup of mascarpone cheese
- 1/2 cup of almond milk
- 1 ½ cup of sugar chips
- Dark chocolate.

Preparation: **Preparation time**: 2 hours

- In a bowl, combine the eggs, honey, vanilla, almonds, and espresso to prepare the ingredients.
- In another bowl, combine the salt, baking soda, and flour of almonds and coconut.
- After adding the wet ingredients to the dry ones, combine all the ingredients.
- Stir in the almond milk.
- Spread the batter into a prepared 8-inch baking dish with coconut oil.
- After 20 to 25 minutes, a toothpick inserted in the center should come out clean.
- Let the cake cool before including the mascarpone cheese and chocolate chips.
- Serve chilled for two hours before serving.

SALAD RECIPES

Greek Cucumber Salad

Ingredients: **Prep time**: 10 minutes

- 1 cup cherry tomatoes, halved;
- 1 cup sliced cucumbers;
- 1/2 cup feta cheese;
- 1/4 cup diced red onion;
- 2 tablespoons extra-virgin olive oil;
- 1 tablespoon red wine vinegar;
- 1/4 teaspoon salt; and
- 1/4 teaspoon freshly ground black pepper.

Preparation: **Preparation time**: 2 minutes

- Combine the cucumbers, tomatoes, feta cheese, and red onion in a big bowl.
- Combine olive oil, red wine vinegar, salt, and pepper in a small bowl.
- Drizzle the salad with the dressing and toss to mix.
- Serve right away.

Avocado Egg Salad

Ingredients: **Prep time**: 10 minutes

- 2 teaspoons Dijon mustard,
- 4 big hard-boiled eggs, chopped;
- 1 large avocado, mashed;
- 2 tablespoons fresh chives, chopped;
- Salt and freshly ground black pepper, to taste.

Preparation: **Preparation time**: 2 minutes

- Combine eggs, avocado, Dijon mustard, and chives in a medium bowl.
- Combine well by mixing.
- To taste, add salt and pepper to the dish.
- Present over a bed of greens, in a wrap, or over toast.

Zucchini Noodle Salad

Ingredients:

- 2 medium spiralized zucchinis,
- 1 cup halved cherry tomatoes,

- 1/4 cup diced red onion,
- 2 tablespoons extra-virgin olive oil,
- 1 tablespoon white wine vinegar,
- 1/4 teaspoon salt, and
- 1/4 teaspoon freshly ground black pepper.

Preparation: **Preparation time**: 2 minutes

- Combine zucchini noodles, cherry tomatoes, and red onion in a big bowl.
- Combine olive oil, white wine vinegar, salt, and pepper in a small bowl.
- Drizzle the salad with the dressing and toss to mix.
- Serve right away.

Chicken Avocado Salad

Ingredients: **Prep time**: 10 minutes

- 1/4 teaspoon salt,
- 1/4 teaspoon freshly ground black pepper,
- 1 cup diced cooked chicken,
- 1 big avocado,
- 1 cup cherry tomatoes, halved,
- 2 tablespoons extra-virgin olive oil.

Preparation: **Preparation time**: 2 minutes

- Combine the chicken, avocado, and cherry tomatoes in a big bowl.

- Combine olive oil, apple cider vinegar, salt, and pepper in a small bowl.
- Drizzle the salad with the dressing and toss to mix.
- Serve right away.

Quinoa Salad

Ingredients: **Prep time**: 10 minutes

- 1 cup cooked quinoa,
- 1/2 cup rinsed and drained black beans,
- 1/2 cup cooked corn,
- 1/2 diced red bell pepper,
- 2 tablespoons extra virgin olive oil,
- 1 tablespoon lime juice,
- 1/4 teaspoon salt, and
- 1/4 teaspoon freshly ground black pepper.

Preparation: **Preparation time**: 2 minutes

- Quinoa, black beans, corn, and red bell pepper should all be combined in a big dish.
- Combine olive oil, lime juice, salt, and pepper in a small bowl.
- Drizzle the salad with the dressing and toss to mix.
- Serve right away.

Tuna Salad

Ingredients: **Prep time**: 10 minutes

- 2 cans of drained tuna;
- 2 celery stalks; one cup of finely chopped red onion;
- 2 tablespoons of extra-virgin olive oil;
- 1 tablespoon of lemon juice;
- ½ teaspoon each of salt and freshly ground black pepper.

Preparation: **Preparation time**: 2 minutes

- Combine the tuna, celery, and red onion in a medium bowl.
- Combine the olive oil, lemon juice, salt, and pepper in a small bowl.
- Drizzle the salad with the dressing and toss to mix.
- Serve right away.

Eggplant Salad

Ingredients: **Prep time**: 10 minutes

- 2 big eggplants, roasted and diced;
- 1 cup cherry tomatoes, halved;
- ½ cup of crumbled feta cheese;
- 2 teaspoons extra-virgin olive oil;
- 1 tablespoon red wine vinegar;
- ¼ teaspoon each of salt and freshly ground black pepper.

Preparation: **Preparation time**: 2 minutes

- Combine the eggplant, tomatoes, and feta cheese in a big bowl.
- Combine olive oil, red wine vinegar, salt, and pepper in a small bowl.
- Drizzle the salad with the dressing and toss to mix.

- Serve right away.

Roasted Veggie Salad

Ingredients: **Prep time**: 10 minutes

- 1 cup cooked quinoa,
- 2 tablespoons extra-virgin olive oil,
- 1 tablespoon balsamic vinegar,
- 1/4 teaspoon salt, and
- 1/4 teaspoon freshly ground black pepper.
- 2 cups chopped roasted veggies, such as potatoes, carrots, onions, and peppers.

Preparation: **Preparation time**: 2 minutes

- Combine quinoa and roasted veggies in a big bowl.
- Combine olive oil, balsamic vinegar, salt, and pepper in a small bowl.
- Drizzle the salad with the dressing and toss to mix.
- Serve right away.

Cauliflower Rice Salad

Ingredients: **Prep time**: 10 minutes

- 2 cups of cauliflower rice,
- 1 cup of finely chopped vegetables (such as peppers, celery, and carrots),
- 2 teaspoons of extra-virgin olive oil,
- 1 tablespoon of apple cider vinegar,

- ¼ teaspoon of salt, and
- ¼ teaspoon of freshly ground black pepper.

Preparation: **Preparation time**: 2 minutes

- Combine cauliflower rice and finely chopped veggies in a large bowl.
- Combine olive oil, apple cider vinegar, salt, and pepper in a small bowl.
- Drizzle the salad with the dressing and toss to mix.
- Serve right away.

Kale Salad

Ingredients: **Prep time**: 10 minutes

- 4 cups chopped kale,
- 1 diced apple,
- 1/4 cup chopped walnuts,
- 2 teaspoons extra virgin olive oil,
- 1 tablespoon apple cider vinegar,
- 1/4 teaspoon salt, and
- 1/4 teaspoon freshly ground black pepper are the

Preparation: **Preparation time**: 2 minutes

- Combine the kale, apple, and walnuts in a big bowl.
- Combine olive oil, apple cider vinegar, salt, and pepper in a small bowl.
- Drizzle the salad with the dressing and toss to mix.

- Serve right away.

Chickpea Salad

Ingredients: **Prep time**: 10 minutes

- 2 cans washed and drained chickpeas,
- 1 cup halved cherry tomatoes,
- 1 cup diced avocado,
- 2 tablespoons extra virgin olive oil,
- 1 tablespoon lemon juice,
- 1/4 teaspoon salt, and
- 1/4 teaspoon freshly ground black pepper.

Preparation: **Preparation time**: 2 minutes

- Combine the chickpeas, avocado, and cherry tomatoes in a big bowl.
- Combine the olive oil, lemon juice, salt, and pepper in a small bowl.
- Drizzle the salad with the dressing and toss to mix.
- Serve right away.

Broccoli Salad

Ingredients: **Prep time**: 10 minutes

- 2 chopped heads of broccoli;
- 1 head of shredded cabbage;
- 1 cup of raisins;
- 2 tablespoons of extra-virgin olive oil;
- 1 tablespoon of apple cider vinegar;

- ¼ teaspoon of salt; and
- ¼ teaspoon of freshly ground black pepper.

Preparation: **Preparation time**: 2 minutes

- Combine broccoli, cabbage, and raisins in a big bowl.
- Combine olive oil, apple cider vinegar, salt, and pepper in a small bowl.
- Drizzle the salad with the dressing and toss to mix.
- Serve right away.

Spinach Salad

Ingredients: **Prep time**: 10 minutes

- 2 teaspoons extra-virgin olive oil,
- 1 tablespoon balsamic vinegar,
- 1/4 teaspoon each of salt and freshly ground black pepper,
- 4 cups chopped spinach,
- 1 cup sliced strawberries,
- 1/4 cup chopped almonds, and
- 2 tablespoons extra-virgin olive oil.

Preparation: **Preparation time**: 2 minutes

- Combine spinach, strawberries, and almonds in a large bowl.
- Combine olive oil, balsamic vinegar, salt, and pepper in a small bowl.
- Drizzle the salad with the dressing and toss to mix.
- Serve right away.

Taco Salad

Ingredients: **Prep time**: 10 minutes

- 2 tablespoons extra virgin olive oil,
- 1 tablespoon lime juice,
- 1/4 teaspoon salt, and
- 1/4 teaspoon freshly ground black pepper.
- 1 pound ground beef,
- 1 can rinse and drained black beans,
- 1 cup halved cherry tomatoes, and
- 2 teaspoons extra virgin olive oil.

Preparation: **Preparation time**: 2 minutes

- Combine ground beef, black beans, and cherry tomatoes in a big bowl.
- Combine olive oil, lime juice, salt, and pepper in a small bowl.
- Drizzle the salad with the dressing and toss to mix.
- Serve right away.

Asparagus Salad

Ingredients: **Prep time**: 10 minutes

- 2 bunches of roasted and chopped asparagus,
- 1 cup of split cherry tomatoes,
- ½ cup of crumbled feta cheese,
- 2 tablespoons of extra-virgin olive oil,
- 1 tablespoon of red wine vinegar,
- 1 teaspoon each of salt and freshly crushed black pepper.

Preparation:

- Combine the asparagus, tomatoes, and feta cheese in a big bowl.

- Combine olive oil, red wine vinegar, salt, and pepper in a small bowl.

- Drizzle the salad with the dressing and toss to mix.

- Serve right away.

Lentil Salad

Ingredients: **Prep time**: 10 minutes

- 2 cups cooked lentils;

- 1 ½ cups chopped bell peppers;

- 1 ¼ cups finely diced red onion;

- 2 tablespoons extra-virgin olive oil;

- 1 tablespoon balsamic vinegar;

- 1 teaspoon salt; and

- 1 and a quarter teaspoons freshly ground black pepper.

Preparation: **Preparation time**: 2 minutes

- To begin, mix the lentils, bell peppers, and red onion in a large bowl.

- Combine olive oil, balsamic vinegar, salt, and pepper in a small bowl.

- Drizzle the salad with the dressing and toss to mix.

- Serve right away.

Delectable salad

Ingredients: **Prep time**: 10 minutes

- 1/4 cup chopped walnuts,
- 2 tablespoons extra virgin olive oil,
- 1 tablespoon white wine vinegar,
- 1/4 teaspoon salt, and
- 1/4 teaspoon freshly ground black pepper.
- 2 cups chopped roasted Brussels sprouts.

Preparation: **Preparation time**: 2 minutes

- Combine the Brussels sprouts and walnuts in a big basin.
- Combine olive oil, white wine vinegar, salt, and pepper in a small bowl.
- Drizzle the salad with the dressing and toss to mix.
- Serve right away.

Cabbage Salad

Ingredients: **Prep time**: 10 minutes

- 1 cup shredded carrots,
- 2 tablespoons apple cider vinegar,
- 1/4 teaspoon salt, and
- 1/4 teaspoon freshly ground black pepper.
- 2 cups shredded cabbage.

Preparation: **Preparation time**: 2 minutes

- Combine the cabbage and carrots in a big basin.

- Combine olive oil, apple cider vinegar, salt, and pepper in a small bowl.
- Drizzle the salad with the dressing and toss to mix.
- Serve right away.

Bean Salad

Ingredients: **Prep time**: 10 minutes

- 2 cans of rinsed and drained beans;
- 1 cup of halved cherry tomatoes;
- 1 tablespoon of finely diced red onion;
- 2 tablespoons of extra-virgin olive oil;
- 1 tablespoon of lime juice;
- ¼ teaspoon each of salt and freshly ground black pepper.

Preparation: **Preparation time**: 2 minutes

- Combine the beans, tomatoes, and red onion in a big bowl.
- Combine olive oil, lime juice, salt, and pepper in a small bowl.
- Drizzle the salad with the dressing and toss to mix.
- Serve right away.

Tomato Salad

Ingredients: **Prep time**: 10 minutes

- 2 tablespoons extra-virgin olive oil,
- 1 tablespoon balsamic vinegar,
- 1/4 teaspoon salt, and

- 1/4 teaspoon freshly ground black pepper.

- 4 cups cherry tomatoes, halved.

- 1/4 cup red onion, finely chopped.

Preparation: **Preparation time**: 2 minutes

- Combine tomatoes and red onion in a big basin.

- Combine olive oil, balsamic vinegar, salt, and pepper in a small bowl.

- Drizzle the salad with the dressing and toss to mix.

- Serve right away.

SNACK RECIPES

Avocado Boats

Ingredients: **Prep time**: 10 minutes

- 2 teaspoons of shredded cheese,
- 2 tablespoons of salsa,
- 1 big avocado,
- 1/2 cup of black beans,
- 1 diced tomato, and
- 1 tablespoon of onion.

Preparation: **Preparation time**: 15 minutes

- Remove the avocado's pit, cut it in half, and scoop out part of the flesh to make room for the filling.

- Combine the black beans, tomato, onion, salsa, and cheese in a small bowl.
- Divide the mixture in half then spoon some into each avocado half.
- Place in the oven for 15 minutes at 350 degrees Fahrenheit.

Kale Chips

Ingredients: **Prep time**: 10 minutes

- 1 bunch of kale,
- 1 tablespoon of olive oil,
- 1/2 teaspoon of garlic powder,
- 1/4 teaspoon of black pepper

Preparation: **Preparation time**: 10 minutes

- Set the oven to 350°F.
- With paper towels, dry the kale leaves after removing them from the stems.
- Add the olive oil, black pepper, and garlic powder to the bowl with the meat.
- Coat by tossing.
- Put the chips on a baking sheet, and bake for 10 minutes, or until crisp.

Avocado Toast

Ingredients: **Prep time**: 5 minutes

- 2 pieces of whole wheat bread,
- ½ an avocado,

- ¼ teaspoon of garlic powder, and
- ¼ teaspoon of black pepper

Preparation: **Preparation time**: 5 minutes

- Avocado is then smeared on top of the toast.
- Garlic powder and black pepper should be added.
- Serve.

Hummus and Veggies

Ingredients: **Prep time**: 5 minutes

- 1/2 cup hummus,
- 1/2 cup bell pepper,
- 1/2 cup carrot, and
- 1/2 cup cucumber slices.

Preparation: **Preparation time**: 5 minutes

- Slices of cucumber, bell pepper, and carrot should be placed on top of the hummus in the bowl.
- Pita chips should be used.

Greek Yogurt Parfait

Ingredients: **Prep time**: 5 minutes

- 1/2 cup blueberries,
- 1/2 cup raspberries,
- 1/4 cup granola,

- 1 cup non-fat Greek yogurt

Preparation: **Preparation time**: 2 minutes

- The yogurt, blueberries, raspberries, and granola should be arranged in a bowl.
- Serve.

Trail Mix

Ingredients: **Prep time**: 5 minutes

- 1/2 cup each of almonds,
- 1/2 walnuts,
- 1/2 dried cranberries, and
- 1/2 dark chocolate chips.

Preparation: **Preparation time**: 2 minutes

- Almonds, walnuts, dried cranberries, and dark chocolate chips should be combined in a dish for preparation.
- Serve.

Apple and Peanut Butter

Ingredients: **Prep time**: 5 minutes

- 1 apple,
- 2 tablespoons of peanut butter,

Preparation: **Preparation time**: 2 minutes

- The peanut butter should be applied to each slice of the cut apple.
- Serve.

Cottage Cheese and Fruit

Ingredients: **Prep time**: 5 minutes

- 1 cup strawberries,
- 1 cup blueberries, and
- 1/2 cup low-fat cottage cheese.

Preparation: **Preparation time**: 2 minutes

- Put the strawberries and blueberries on top of the cottage cheese in the bowl.
- Serve.

Roasted Chickpeas

Ingredients: **Prep time**: 10 minutes

- 1 can chickpeas,
- 2 tablespoons olive oil,
- 1/4 teaspoon black pepper,

Preparation: **Preparation time**: 10 minutes

- Turn on the 375°F oven.
- Chickpeas should be drained and rinsed.
- Add the olive oil, black pepper, and garlic powder to the bowl with the meat.

- Coat by tossing. Bake for 10 minutes, or until the chickpeas are crispy, on a baking sheet.
- Serve.

Edamame

Ingredients: **Prep time**: 5 minutes

- 1 cup of edamame,
- 1/4 teaspoon sea salt

Preparation: **Preparation time**: 5 minutes

- Water should be heated up in a saucepan.
- Boil the edamame for 5 minutes after adding it.
- After draining, sea salt should be added.
- Serve.

Guacamole and Veggies

Ingredients: **Prep time**: 5 minutes

- 1/2 cup guacamole,
- 1/2 cup carrots,
- 1/2 cup cherry tomatoes, and
- 1/2 cup bell peppers.

Preparation: **Preparation time**: 5 minutes

- Bell peppers, carrots, and cherry tomatoes should be placed on top of the guacamole in the bowl.

- Pita chips should be used.

Turkey wraps

Ingredients: **Prep time**: 5 minutes

- 2 whole wheat tortillas,
- 1/2 cup sliced turkey,
- 1/2 cup lettuce,
- 1/4 cup tomatoes.

Preparation: **Preparation time**: 5 minutes

- On the tortillas, arrange the turkey, lettuce, and tomatoes.
- Wrap up and dish out.

Berry Smoothie

Ingredients: **Prep time**: 5 minutes

- 1 cup of frozen strawberries,
- 1 cup of frozen blueberries,
- 1 cup of almond milk, and
- 1/2 teaspoon of honey.

Preparation: **Preparation time**: 2 minutes

- Blend each item in the blender until it is smooth.
- Serve.

Cucumber Slices with Hummus

Ingredients: **Prep time**: 5 minutes

- 1 cucumber,
- 1/2 cup hummus,

Preparation: **Preparation time**: 2 minutes

- Slice the cucumber into thin pieces before cooking.
- Serve with hummus.

Quinoa Bowl

Ingredients: **Prep time**: 10 minutes

- 1/2 cup cooked quinoa,
- 1/2 cup black beans,
- 1/2 cup corn,
- 1/4 cup red onion,
- 1/4 cup olive oil,
- 1/4 teaspoon garlic powder, and
- 1/4 teaspoon black pepper.

Preparation: **Preparation time**: minutes

- Quinoa, black beans, corn, tomatoes, and red onion should all be combined in a bowl.
- Add the black pepper, garlic powder, and olive oil.
- Mix ingredients with dressing in a bowl.

Avocado Egg Toast

Ingredients: **Prep time**: 5 minutes

- 2 pieces of whole wheat bread,

- 1/2 avocado,

- 2 hard-boiled eggs.

Preparation: **Preparation time**: 5 minutes

- Toast bread before spreading the avocado on it.

- Add the cooked eggs on top. Serve.

Popcorn

Ingredients: **Prep time**: 5 minutes

- 1/4 teaspoon sea salt,

- 1/2 cup popcorn kernels,

- 2 tablespoons olive oil

Preparation: **Preparation time**: 5 minutes

- Over medium heat, warm the olive oil in a big saucepan.

- Cover after adding the popcorn kernels.

- Until the popcorn is popped, shake the pot periodically.

- Serve after seasoning with sea salt.

Turkey and Cheese Roll-Ups

Ingredients: **Prep time**: 5 minutes

- 2 slices of turkey,

- 2 pieces of cheese,

- 2 whole wheat tortillas

Preparation: **Preparation time**: 5 minutes

- Put the cheese and turkey on the tortillas.
- Wrap up and dish out.

Fruit Skewers

Ingredients: **Prep time**: 5 minutes

- One cup of strawberries,
- one cup of pineapple, and
- half a cup of blueberries

Preparation: **Preparation time**: 2 minutes

- Strawberries, pineapple, and blueberries are threaded onto skewers.
- Serve.

Asparagus fries

Ingredients: **Prep time**: 5 minutes

- 1 bunch asparagus,
- 1 tablespoon olive oil,
- 1/4 teaspoon garlic powder,
- 1/4 teaspoon black pepper.

Preparation: **Preparation time**: 10 minutes

- Turn on the 375°F oven.
- The asparagus should be thinly sliced.

- Add the olive oil, black pepper, and garlic powder to the bowl with the meat.

- Coat by tossing. Put the fries in the oven for 10 minutes, or until they are crisp.

- Serve.

SOUP RECIPES

Garden Vegetable Soup

Ingredients:

Prep time: 10 minutes

- 1/2 cup of green beans,

- 2 cups of vegetable broth,

- 1/4 cup of parsley,

- 1/4 teaspoon each of thyme, oregano, and basil,

- 1 onion,

- 1 garlic clove,
- 2 stalks of celery,
- 1 carrot.
- Salt and pepper to flavor
- 2 teaspoons of olive oil.

Preparation: **Preparation time**: 20 minutes

- In a large saucepan set over medium-high heat, warm the olive oil.
- For approximately 5 minutes, add the onion and garlic and simmer until tender.
- Green beans, celery, and carrot should all be added now and cooked for approximately 5 minutes or until tender.
- Bring to a boil the vegetable broth together with the parsley, thyme, oregano, basil, salt, and pepper.
- Simmer for 10 minutes on low heat.
- Serve warm.

Tomato Soup

Ingredients: **Prep time**: 10 minutes

- 2 tablespoons of extra virgin olive oil,
- 1 onion, 2 cloves of garlic,
- 2 cans of diced tomatoes,
- 2 cups of vegetable broth,
- 1 teaspoon each of oregano and basil pepper and salt as desired

Preparation: **Preparation time**: 25 minutes

- In a large saucepan set over medium-high heat, warm the olive oil.
- For approximately 5 minutes, add the onion and garlic and simmer until tender.
- Bring to a boil after adding the tomatoes and vegetable broth. Simmer for 10 minutes on low heat.
- Simmer for a further 10 minutes after adding the oregano, basil, salt, and pepper to taste. Serve warm.

Chicken soup

Ingredients: **Prep time**: 10 minutes

- 2 tablespoons of olive oil,
- 1 onion,
- 2 garlic cloves,
- 2 cups of shredded chicken,
- 4 cups of chicken stock,
- 1/2 cup of chopped celery,
- 1/2 cup of chopped carrots,
- 1/2 cup of frozen peas,
- 1 teaspoon each of oregano and basil, pepper and salt as desired

Preparation: **Preparation time**: 25 minutes

- In a large saucepan set over medium-high heat, warm the olive oil.

- For approximately 5 minutes, add the onion and garlic and simmer until tender.

- Bring to a boil the shredded chicken, chicken stock, celery, carrots, and frozen peas.

- Simmer for ten minutes on low heat.

- Simmer for a further 10 minutes after adding the oregano, basil, salt, and pepper to taste.

- Serve warm.

Split-pea soup

Ingredients: **Prep time**: 10 minutes

- 2 tablespoons of olive oil,
- 1 onion,
- 2 garlic cloves,
- 1 cup of split peas,
- 4 cups of vegetable broth,
- 1/2 cup of chopped carrots,
- 1/2 cup of chopped celery,
- 1 teaspoon each of oregano and basil, pepper and salt as desired

Preparation: **Preparation time**: 25 minutes

- In a large saucepan set over medium-high heat, warm the olive oil.
- For approximately 5 minutes, add the onion and garlic and simmer until tender.
- Bring to a boil the split peas, vegetable broth, carrots, and celery.

- Simmer for 10 minutes on low heat.
- Simmer for a further 10 minutes after adding the oregano, basil, salt, and pepper to taste.
- Serve warm.

Mushroom Soup

Ingredients: **Prep time**: 10 minutes

- 1 onion,
- 2 cloves of garlic,
- 16 ounces of fresh mushrooms,
- 4 cups of vegetable stock,
- 1/2 cup of chopped celery,
- 1/2 cup of chopped carrots,
- 1 teaspoon of oregano,
- 1 teaspoon of basil, salt, and pepper to taste

Preparation: **Preparation time**: 25 minutes

- In a large saucepan set over medium-high heat, warm the olive oil.
- For approximately 5 minutes, add the onion and garlic and simmer until tender.
- Bring to a boil after adding the mushrooms, vegetable broth, celery, and carrots.
- Simmer for ten minutes on low heat.
- Simmer for a further 10 minutes after adding the oregano, basil, salt, and pepper to taste. Serve warm.

Green lentil soup

Ingredients: **Prep time**: 10 minutes

- 4 cups of vegetable broth,
- 1/2 cup of chopped celery,
- 1/2 cup of chopped carrots,
- 1 teaspoon each of oregano and basil,
- 2 tablespoons of olive oil,
- 1 onion,
- 2 cloves of garlic,
- 1 cup of green lentils, pepper and salt as desired

Preparation: **Preparation time**: 25 minutes

- In a large saucepan set over medium-high heat, warm the olive oil.
- For approximately 5 minutes, add the onion and garlic and simmer until tender.
- Bring to a boil after adding the lentils, vegetable broth, celery, and carrots.
- Simmer for 10 minutes on low heat.
- Simmer for a further 10 minutes after adding the oregano, basil, salt, and pepper to taste. Serve warm.

Minestrone Soup

Ingredients: **Prep time**: 10 minutes

- 2 tablespoons olive oil,
- 1 onion,

- 2 garlic cloves,
- 1 can diced tomatoes,
- 2 cups vegetable broth,
- 1 cup chopped carrots,
- 1 cup diced celery,
- 1 cup cooked beans,
- 1 teaspoon oregano,
- 1 teaspoon basil, salt, and pepper to taste

Preparation: **Preparation time**: 25 minutes

- In a large saucepan set over medium-high heat, warm the olive oil.
- For approximately 5 minutes, add the onion and garlic and simmer until tender.
- Bring to a boil after adding the chopped tomatoes, vegetable broth, carrots, celery, and beans.
- Simmer for 10 minutes on low heat.
- Simmer for a further 10 minutes after adding the oregano, basil, salt, and pepper to taste.
- Serve warm.

Cabbage Soup

Ingredients: **Prep time**: 10 minutes

- 2 tablespoons of extra virgin olive oil,
- 1 onion,
- 2 cloves of garlic,

- 2 cups of shredded cabbage,
- 4 cups of vegetable broth,
- 1/2 cup of chopped celery,
- 1/2 cup of chopped carrots,
- 1 teaspoon each of oregano and basil, salt and pepper to taste.

Preparation: **Preparation time**: 25 minutes

- In a large saucepan set over medium-high heat, warm the olive oil.
- For approximately 5 minutes, add the onion and garlic and simmer until tender.
- Bring to a boil after adding the shredded cabbage, vegetable broth, celery, and carrots.
- Simmer for 10 minutes on low heat.
- Simmer for a further 10 minutes after adding the oregano, basil, salt, and pepper to taste.
- Serve warm.

Broccoli soup

Ingredients: **Prep time**: 10 minutes

- 1 onion,
- 2 cloves of garlic,
- 2 cups of fresh broccoli florets,
- 4 cups of vegetable stock,
- 1/2 cup of chopped celery,
- 1/2 cup of chopped carrots,

- 1 teaspoon each of oregano and basil, salt and pepper to taste

Preparation: **Preparation time**: 25 minutes

- In a large saucepan set over medium-high heat, warm the olive oil.
- For approximately 5 minutes, add the onion and garlic and simmer until tender.
- Bring to a boil after adding the broccoli, vegetable broth, celery, and carrots.
- Simmer for 10 minutes on low heat.
- Simmer for a further 10 minutes after adding the oregano, basil, salt, and pepper to taste.
- Serve warm.

Tuscan Bean Soup

Ingredients: **Prep time**: 10 minutes

- 2 tablespoons olive oil,
- 1 onion,
- 2 garlic cloves,
- 1 can of cannellini beans,
- 4 cups of vegetable broth,
- 1/2 cup chopped celery,
- 1/2 cup chopped carrots,
- 1 teaspoon each of oregano, basil, and rosemary. pepper and salt as desired

Preparation: **Preparation time**: 25 minutes

- In a large saucepan set over medium-high heat, warm the olive oil.
- For approximately 5 minutes, add the onion and garlic and simmer until tender.
- Bring to a boil after adding the cannellini beans, vegetable broth, celery, carrots, oregano, basil, and rosemary.
- Simmer for 10 minutes on low heat.
- Simmer for a further 10 minutes after adding the salt and pepper to taste.
- Serve warm.

Cauliflower soup

Ingredients: **Prep time**: 10 minutes

- 2 tablespoons olive oil,
- 1 onion,
- 2 cloves of garlic,
- 2 cups of finely chopped cauliflower florets,
- 4 cups of vegetable broth,
- 1/2 cup of finely chopped celery,
- 1/2 cup of finely chopped carrots,
- 1 teaspoon each of oregano and basil, and salt and pepper to taste

Preparation: **Preparation time**: 25 minutes

- In a large saucepan set over medium-high heat, warm the olive oil.

- For approximately 5 minutes, add the onion and garlic and simmer until tender.
- Bring to a boil after adding the cauliflower, vegetable broth, celery, and carrots.
- Simmer for 10 minutes on low heat.
- Simmer for a further 10 minutes after adding the oregano, basil, salt, and pepper to taste.
- Serve warm.

Zucchini Soup

Ingredients: **Prep time**: 10 minutes

- 1 onion,
- 2 cloves of garlic,
- 2 cups of chopped zucchini,
- 4 cups of vegetable stock,
- 1/2 cup of chopped celery,
- 1/2 cup of chopped carrots,
- 1 teaspoon each of oregano and basil, and salt and pepper to taste

Preparation: **Preparation time**: 25 minutes

- In a large saucepan set over medium-high heat, warm the olive oil.
- For approximately 5 minutes, add the onion and garlic and simmer until tender.
- Bring to a boil after adding the zucchini, vegetable broth, celery, and carrots.

- Simmer for 10 minutes on low heat.

- Simmer for a further 10 minutes after adding the oregano, basil, salt, and pepper to taste.

- Serve warm.

Barley Soup

Ingredients: **Prep time**: 10 minutes

- 4 cups of vegetable broth,

- 1/2 cup of chopped celery,

- 1/2 cup of chopped carrots,

- 1 teaspoon each of oregano and basil,

- 2 tablespoons of olive oil,

- 1 onion,

- 2 cloves of garlic,

- 1 cup of barley, pepper, and salt as desired

Preparation: **Preparation time**: 25 minutes

- In a large saucepan set over medium-high heat, warm the olive oil.

- For approximately 5 minutes, add the onion and garlic and simmer until tender.

- Bring to a boil after adding the barley, vegetable broth, celery, and carrots.

- Simmer for 10 minutes on low heat.

- Simmer for a further 10 minutes after adding the oregano, basil, salt, and pepper to taste.

- Serve warm.

Spinach Soup

Ingredients: **Prep time**: 10 minutes

- 4 cups of vegetable broth,
- 2 tablespoons of olive oil,
- 1 onion,
- 2 cloves of garlic,
- 2 cups of fresh spinach,
- 1/2 cup of chopped celery,
- 1/2 cup of chopped carrots,
- 1 teaspoon each of oregano and basil, pepper and salt as desired

Preparation: **Preparation time**: 25 minutes

- In a large saucepan set over medium-high heat, warm the olive oil.
- For approximately 5 minutes, add the onion and garlic and simmer until tender.
- Bring to a boil after adding the spinach, vegetable broth, celery, and carrots.
- Simmer for 10 minutes on low heat.
- Simmer for a further 10 minutes after adding the oregano, basil, salt, and pepper to taste.
- Serve warm.

Coconut Milk Soup

Ingredients: **Prep time**: 10 minutes

- 2 tablespoons coconut oil,
- 1 onion,
- 2 garlic cloves,
- 2 cups coconut milk,
- 4 cups vegetable broth,
- 1/2 cup chopped celery,
- 1/2 cup chopped carrots,
- 1 teaspoon oregano,
- 1 teaspoon basil, salt, and pepper to taste

Preparation: **Preparation time**: 25 minutes

- In a large saucepan set over medium-high heat, warm the coconut oil.
- For approximately 5 minutes, add the onion and garlic and simmer until tender.
- Bring to a boil after adding the coconut milk, vegetable broth, celery, and carrots.
- Simmer for 10 minutes on low heat.
- Simmer for a further 10 minutes after adding the oregano, basil, salt, and pepper to taste.
- Serve warm.

Carrot Soup

Ingredients: **Prep time**: 10 minutes

- 4 cups of vegetable broth,
- 1/2 cup of chopped celery,
- 1/2 cup of chopped onions,
- 1 teaspoon each of oregano and basil,
- 2 teaspoons of olive oil,
- 1 onion,
- 2 cloves of garlic, and
- 2 cups of chopped carrots. pepper and salt as desired

Preparation: **Preparation time**: 25 minutes

- In a large saucepan set over medium-high heat, warm the olive oil.
- For approximately 5 minutes, add the onion and garlic and simmer until tender.
- Bring to a boil after adding the carrots, vegetable broth, celery, and onions.
- Simmer for 10 minutes on low heat.
- Simmer for a further 10 minutes after adding the oregano, basil, salt, and pepper to taste.
- Serve warm.

Broccoli and cheddar soup

Ingredients: **Prep time**: 10 minutes

- 1 onion,
- 2 garlic cloves,
- 2 cups of chopped broccoli,

- 4 cups of vegetable broth,
- 1/2 cup of cheddar cheese,
- 1/2 cup of milk,
- 1 teaspoon each of oregano and basil pepper and salt as desired

Preparation: **Preparation time**: 25 minutes

- In a large saucepan set over medium-high heat, melt the butter.
- For approximately 5 minutes, add the onion and garlic and simmer until tender.
- Bring to a boil after adding the broccoli, vegetable broth, cheddar cheese, and milk.
- Simmer for 10 minutes on low heat.
- Simmer for a further 10 minutes after adding the oregano, basil, salt, and pepper to taste.
- Serve warm.

Creamy mushroom soup

Ingredients: **Prep time**: 10 minutes

- 2 tablespoons butter,
- 1 onion,
- 2 cloves of garlic,
- 16 ounces of fresh mushrooms,
- 4 cups of vegetable stock,
- 1/2 cup of cream,
- 1 teaspoon each of oregano and basil pepper, and salt as desired

Preparation: **Preparation time**: 25 minutes

- In a large saucepan set over medium-high heat, melt the butter.
- For approximately 5 minutes, add the onion and garlic and simmer until tender.
- Bring to a boil after adding the mushrooms, vegetable broth, and cream.
- Simmer for 10 minutes on low heat.
- Simmer for a further 10 minutes after adding the oregano, basil, salt, and pepper to taste.
- Serve warm.

Sweet Potato Soup

Ingredients: **Prep time**: 10 minutes

- 2 tablespoons of olive oil,
- 1 onion,
- 2 garlic cloves,
- 2 cups of finely diced sweet potatoes,
- 4 cups of vegetable broth,
- 1/2 cup of finely chopped celery,
- 1/2 cup of finely chopped carrots,
- 1 teaspoon each of oregano and basil, salt and pepper to taste

Preparation: **Preparation time**: 25 minutes

- In a large saucepan set over medium-high heat, warm the olive oil.

- For approximately 5 minutes, add the onion and garlic and simmer until tender.

- Bring to a boil after adding the sweet potatoes, vegetable broth, celery, and carrots.

- Simmer for 10 minutes on low heat.

- Simmer for a further 10 minutes after adding the oregano, basil, salt, and pepper to taste.

- Serve warm.

Butternut squash soup

Ingredients: **Prep time**: 10 minutes

- 2 tablespoons of olive oil,

- 1 onion, 2 cloves of garlic,

- 2 cups of finely diced butternut squash,

- 4 cups of vegetable broth,

- 1 teaspoon each of oregano and basil, salt, and pepper to taste

Preparation: **Preparation time**: 25 minutes

- In a large saucepan set over medium-high heat, warm the olive oil.

- For approximately 5 minutes, add the onion and garlic and simmer until tender.

- Bring to a boil after adding the butternut squash, vegetable broth, celery, and carrots.

- Simmer for 10 minutes on low heat.

- Simmer for a further 10 minutes after adding the oregano, basil, salt, and pepper to taste.
- Serve warm.

PROS AND CONS OF THE LOW CARB HIGH FIBER COOKBOOK

A collection of dishes intended to be high in fiber and low in carbs may be found in the Low Carb High Fiber Cookbook.

Here are some pros and cons of utilizing this cookbook:

Pros:

1. This Low Carb High Fiber Cookbook offers a wide variety of meals that are delicious and nutritious. Recipes are simple to follow and may be made using common items.

2. These recipes were created especially for those who follow a low-carb and high-fiber diet. They are not only appropriate for those who are attempting to reduce weight, but they may also provide people who need to maintain a healthy lifestyle.

3. The cookbook includes several recipes that may be adapted to fit different dietary requirements, such as vegetarian, vegan, gluten-free, and dairy-free alternatives.

4. The book is chock with nutritional knowledge that may assist readers in making wise eating decisions.

5. The cookbook offers useful hints and techniques for preparing meals that are both healthier and more delectable.

6. **Weight loss**: Recipes in a cookbook called Low Carb High Fiber are designed to be low in carbs, which may aid in weight loss. These meals may aid in lowering total calorie intake, which can result in weight loss, by minimizing the consumption of carbs.

7. **Improved Blood Sugar Control**: It has been shown that low-carb, high-fiber diets help diabetics control their blood sugar levels. People with diabetes may benefit from these recipes' ability to maintain stable blood sugar levels.

8. **Increased Fiber intake**: High-fiber diets may aid in promoting feelings of fullness and reducing hunger, which can be advantageous for weight loss and general health.

9. **Recipe diversity**: A Low Carb High Fiber cookbook usually offers a range of recipes, including main meals, sides, snacks, and desserts, which may make meal planning and preparation simpler.

10. **Nutrient-dense**: Providing a solid mix of necessary vitamins, minerals, and other nutrients, low-carb, high-fiber dishes are often nutrient-dense.

Cons:

1. **Limited food choices**: Limitations on some foods, such as grains, fruits, and sweets, may make it challenging for some individuals to maintain a low-carb, high-fiber diet.

2. **Diet difficulty**: The diet may be challenging for certain individuals, particularly those who are accustomed to eating a diet heavy in carbs.

3. **Time spent cooking**: Some dishes may take longer to make than others, which may be a problem for those with hectic schedules.

4. **Limited options for vegetarians**: Since some of the cookbook's recipes may include meat, fowl, or fish, they may not be acceptable for vegetarians.

5. **Potential Nutrient deficiencies**: Potential nutritional deficits might result from restricting particular meals if it is not carefully planned and balanced.

In conclusion, this cookbook called Low Carb Rich Fiber may provide a range of recipes that are low in carbs and high in fiber. These dishes can help with weight loss, better blood sugar control, and increased fiber consumption, among other health benefits. Before beginning any new diet, it's crucial to speak with a medical practitioner to be sure it's suitable for your requirements and that any possible nutritional shortages are taken care of.

CONCLUSION

In conclusion, The Low Carb High Fiber Cookbook is a helpful tool for anybody wishing to increase their consumption of fiber and decrease their intake of carbohydrates to enhance their health and general well-being.

The cookbook is brimming with a broad range of delicious and healthful dishes that are simple to make and pleasurable to consume. Making the appropriate food choices, which are essential to a healthy diet and way of life, will be aided by the cookbook. You will find it simple to plan and make meals with the aid of this cookbook that will both satisfy your palate and feed your health.

The cookbook is an excellent resource for discovering the benefits of a low-carb, high-fiber diet and how to apply it to your everyday routine. You may easily make your meals using the recipes' simple-to-follow directions and step-by-step images. You will have a wide range of alternatives to pick from, so whether you like vegetarianism or meat, breakfast, lunch, dinner, snacks, or desserts, you may discover a dish that appeals to you.

For anybody trying to enhance their health and well-being via food, this Low Carb High Fiber cookbook is a must. This cookbook is guaranteed to assist you in achieving your health objectives while enjoying tasty and fulfilling meals with its mouthwatering and nutritious recipes, simple-to-follow directions, and recommendations.

So this cookbook is an excellent place to start if you want to improve your diet and lifestyle for the better. With its assistance, you may anticipate a future filled with tasty and nourishing meals that are both pleasant and healthy.

Made in the USA
Monee, IL
10 October 2023